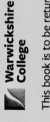
Moreton Morrell Site

Claus Mattheck

Tree Mechanics

Explained with Sensitive Words By Pauli the Bear

1st Edition

DRAWINGS AND TEXT: CLAUS MATTHECK
LETTERING AND LAYOUT: JUERGEN SCHAEFER
TRANSLATION: WILLIAM LINNARD

(c) 2002 BY FORSCHUNGSZENTRUM KARLSRUHE GMBH
POSTFACH 3640, D-76021 KARLSRUHE
ISBN 3-923704-40-2

CONTENTS

III

VI

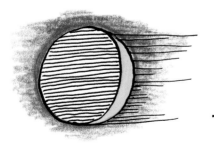

FOR LEO
THE STEALTHY QUESTING SPIRIT
WHO OFTEN FOLLOWED ME
IN THE DARK FIR FOREST
FLEET OF FOOT
ON COOL MOSS
WHERE THE ELVES REST
AT NIGHT
WHEN THE NEW MOON
IS MIRRORED
IN THE EYES OF THE
BANISHED BULL TERRIER –
FOR LEO LION-HEART

$$\tau = \frac{Q}{\pi R^2}$$

2

HELLO FRIENDS, I AM PAULI - THE BEAR. I'M NOW GOING TO SHOW YOU SOME MECHANICS, NOT EVERYTHING OF COURSE, BUT QUITE A LOT WHICH WILL HELP US TO A BETTER UNDERSTANDING OF TREES AND THEIR BURDENS. I'M ALSO GOING TO SHOW YOU A FEW SIMPLE FORMULAE. WITH A SMALL POCKET CALCULATOR YOU CAN THEN WORK OUT LOADS IN TREES YOURSELF. BUT YOU MAY JUST LOOK AT THE DRAWINGS AND SIMPLY IGNORE THE FORMULAE. IN THIS WAY YOU CAN VISUALIZE THE MECHANICAL CONCEPTS. PERHAPS YOU WILL THEN TRY THE FORMULAE LATER - IT'S QUITE EASY - JUST FOLLOW ME! FOLLOW PAULI THE BEAR!

3

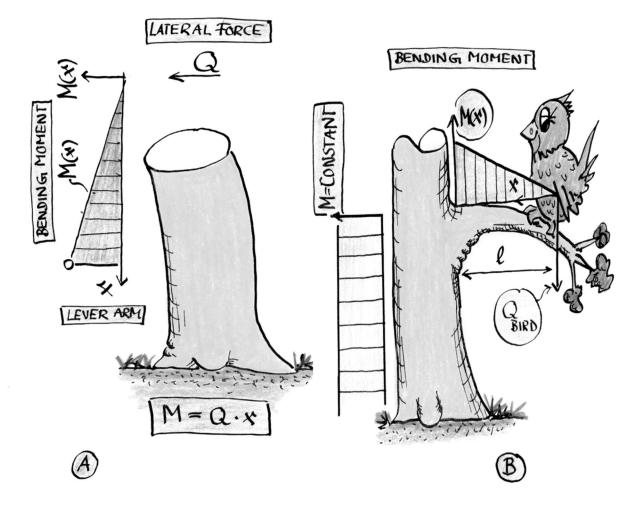

4

$$M = Q \cdot \ell$$

BENDING MOMENT = FORCE × LEVER ARM

WHEN A FORCE Q PRESSES TRANSVERSELY ON A TREE STEM (A), IT PRODUCES A BENDING MOMENT $M = Q \cdot x$ AT A DISTANCE x FROM THE FORCE. THE BENDING MOMENT THUS INCREASES WITH INCREASING DISTANCE FROM THE FORCE. BUT: IF A BRANCH IS BENT DOWN BY A REALLY HEAVY BIRD (B), THEN THE BENDING MOMENT IN THE BRANCH ALSO INCREASES TOWARDS THE STEM. BUT BECAUSE THE BRANCH IS ATTACHED TO THE STEM, THE STEM MUST CONDUCT THE MAXIMUM BRANCH BENDING MOMENT $M = Q_{BIRD} \cdot \ell$ INTO THE GROUND. IF NOTHING ELSE IS BENDING THE STEM, THE BENDING MOMENT IS CONSTANT THERE!

M_T

$M_T = \text{CONSTANT}$

Q

D

$\downarrow x$

$M_{B(x)}$

$M_B = Q \cdot x$

$\downarrow x$

Q

D

M_T

$M_T = \text{CONSTANT}$

$\downarrow x$

PURE TORSION	
$M_T = Q \cdot D$	$M_B = 0$

TORSION AND BENDING	
$M_T = Q \cdot D$	$M_B = Q \cdot x$

6

THE TORSIONAL MOMENT M_T IS ALSO FORCE · LEVERARM , EXACTLY THE SAME AS THE BENDING MOMENT. IF THERE IS A PAIR OF FORCES AT A DISTANCE D FROM EACH OTHER, THEN THE TWO FORCES WILL TWIST THE STEM IN THE SAME DIRECTION. BUT AS ONE OF THE PAIR OF FORCES IS TRYING TO BEND THE STEM FORWARDS AND THE OTHER BACKWARDS, THEY DO NOT BEND THE STEM AT ALL BUT MERELY TWIST IT.

THE TORSIONAL LEVER-ARM IS CONSTANT, AND THEREFORE THE TORSIONAL MOMENT IS EQUALLY GREAT EVERYWHERE IN THE STEM, VIZ $M_T = Q \cdot D$. THINGS ARE RATHER DIFFERENT IN THE RIGHT-HAND PICTURE. THERE A FORCE IS ACTING ON THE LEVER D AND IS TWISTING THE TREE. BUT THIS SAME FORCE IS ALSO ACTING ON THE DOWNWARD POINTING LEVER-ARM x AND BENDING THE TREE. THE BENDING MOMENT INCREASES DOWNWARDS. ITS HIGHEST VALUE $M_B = Q \cdot \ell$ IS DOWN AT THE STEM BASE. THAT'S WHY TREES ARE BROAD AT THE BASE! THE CASE ON THE RIGHT IS OFTEN FOUND IN TREES WHICH HAVE A LOP-SIDED CROWN. THEY ARE BENT AND TWISTED.

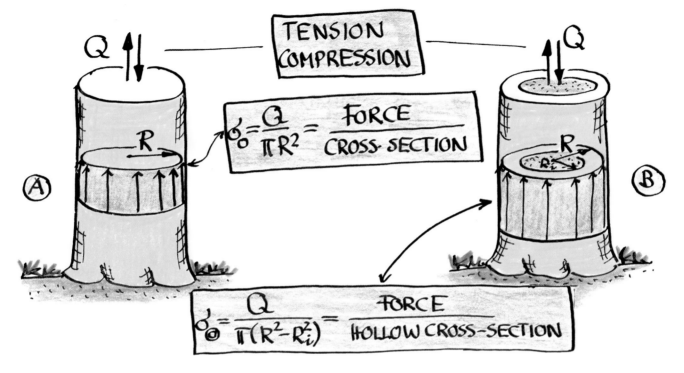

$$\text{TENSION} \atop \text{COMPRESSION}$$

$$\sigma_0 = \frac{Q}{\pi R^2} = \frac{\text{FORCE}}{\text{CROSS-SECTION}}$$

$$\sigma_0 = \frac{Q}{\pi (R^2 - R_i^2)} = \frac{\text{FORCE}}{\text{HOLLOW CROSS-SECTION}}$$

HERE THE LONGITUDINAL FORCES Q (EITHER TENSION OR COMPRESSION, NOT BOTH TOGETHER AS DRAWN!) ARE ACTING IN THE MIDDLE OF THE STEM WITHOUT A LEVER-ARM. ACCORDINGLY THERE IS NEITHER A BENDING MOMENT NOR A TORSIONAL MOMENT HERE. WITH A LONGITUDINAL COMPRESSIVE FORCE, E.G. THE WEIGHT OF THE CROWN, COMPRESSIVE STRESSES OCCUR IN THE STEM, WHICH ARE DISTRIBUTED UNIFORMLY OVER THE STEM.

8

TENSION↑ ↓COMPRESSION

THE STRESSES ARE LONGITUDINAL FORCE / CROSS-SECTION. IF THEY ARE TENSILE FORCES, TENSILE STRESSES WILL OCCUR. BUT THE FORMULA IS THE SAME. IF IT IS A HOLLOW TREE, THEN THE STRESS IS NATURALLY GREATER, FOR THEN IT EQUALS LONGITUDINAL FORCE / HOLLOW CROSS-SECTION. WITH THE HOLLOW TREE YOU MUST IMAGINE THAT THE LONGITUDINAL FORCE IS ACTING IN THE MIDDLE OF A COVER LYING ON TOP OF THE HOLLOW TREE, BECAUSE NO LOAD CAN BE INDUCED IN THE MIDDLE OF THE CAVITY. INTERNAL COMPRESSIVE STRESSES ARE THE STEM'S RESISTANCE AGAINST SHORTENING, AND TENSILE STRESSES AGAINST STRETCHING. THE STRUCTURE DEFENDS ITSELF AGAINST DEFOR-MATION. FOR EXAMPLE, THE WEIGHT OF THE TREE'S CROWN IS A LONGITUDINAL COMPRESSIVE FORCE DOWNWARDS.

9

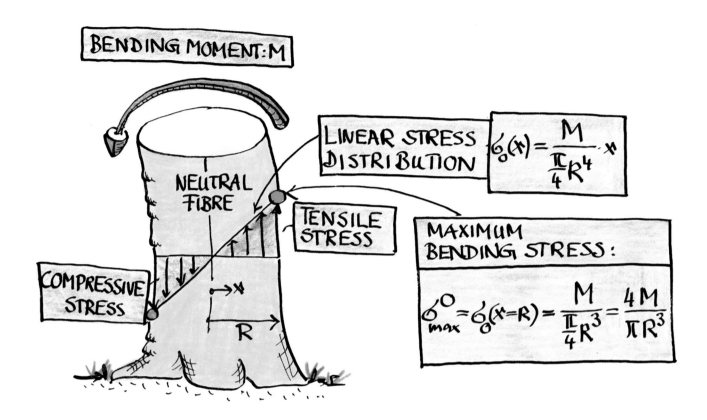

BENDING MOMENT: M

NEUTRAL FIBRE

LINEAR STRESS DISTRIBUTION

$$\sigma_0(x) = \frac{M}{\frac{\pi}{4}R^4} \cdot x$$

TENSILE STRESS

COMPRESSIVE STRESS

MAXIMUM BENDING STRESS:

$$\sigma_{max}^0 = \sigma_0(x=R) = \frac{M}{\frac{\pi}{4}R^3} = \frac{4M}{\pi R^3}$$

THE RINGS ◯ REPRESENT STRESSES IN THE SOLID STEM.

10

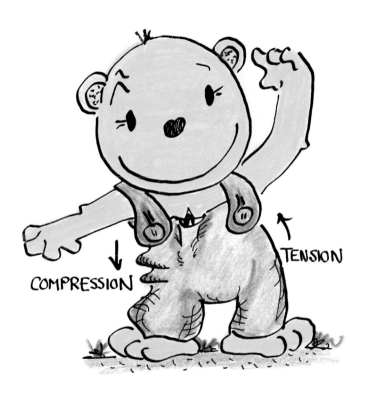

COMPRESSION

TENSION

THE BENDING MOMENTS ALSO PRODUCE STRESSES IN THE TREE, I.E. BENDING STRESSES. THESE ARE COMPRESSIVE STRESSES ON ONE SIDE OF THE TREE WHICH BECOMES SHORTER WITH BENDING, AND TENSILE STRESSES ON THE OTHER SIDE OF THE TREE WHICH BECOMES LONGER WITH BENDING. IN THE MIDDLE, ON THE NEUTRAL FIBRE, THE BENDING STRESSES ARE EQUAL TO ZERO. THE STEM RADIUS IS INVOLVED IN THE BENDING STRESSES AS R^3. THIS MEANS THAT A TREE HAVING THE SAME BENDING MOMENT BUT ONLY HALF THE DIAMETER WILL HAVE BENDING STRESSES 8 TIMES GREATER. THAT'S WHY HUNDREDS OF POLE-SIZE TREES BREAK WHEN THE WIND GETS INTO THE STAND.

11

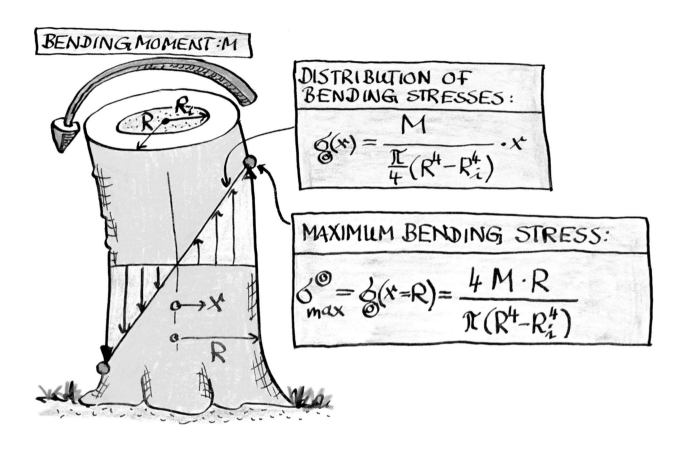

THE RINGS ⊙ INDICATE STRESSES IN THE HOLLOW STEM.

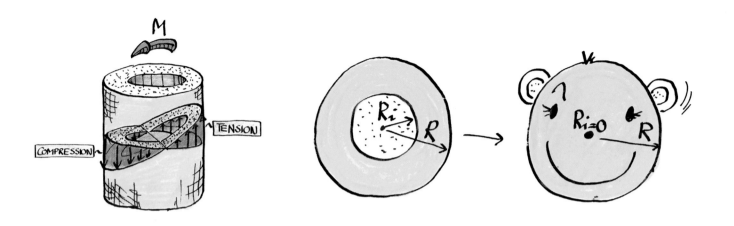

THE LINEAR STRESS DISTRIBUTION IS ACTUALLY ONLY A SIDE VIEW. CONSIDERED SPATIALLY, THE BENDING STRESSES NATURALLY LOOK LIKE THOSE ABOVE (LEFT), FOR NO STRESSES CAN ACT IN THE CAVITY. NATURALLY, THE BENDING STRESSES WILL ALSO BE SOMEWHAT GREATER IN HOLLOW TREES. BUT THEY ONLY BEGIN TO INCREASE SIGNIFICANTLY WHEN THE TREE IS WELL OVER 70% HOLLOW. BECAUSE THE BENDING STRESSES IN THE MIDDLE OF THE STEM ARE EQUAL TO ZERO, IT'S NOT SO BAD IF THIS MIDDLE PART IS HOLLOW. IF YOU PUT THE INTERNAL RADIUS $R_i = 0$, THE FORMULA AGAIN BECOMES THE SAME AS FOR THE SOLID STEM.

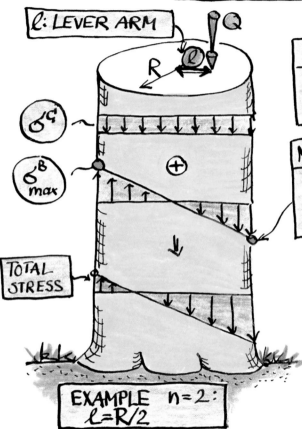

ℓ: LEVER ARM

Q

R ℓ

σ^c

σ^B_{max}

$\oplus$

TOTAL STRESS

COMPRESSIVE STRESS

$$\sigma^c = \frac{Q}{\pi \cdot R^2}$$

MAXIMUM BENDING STRESS

$$\sigma^B_{max} = \frac{4 \cdot M}{\pi \cdot R^3} = \frac{4 \cdot Q \cdot \ell}{\pi \cdot R^3}$$

WITH $\ell = R/n$ FOLLOWS

$$\frac{\sigma^B_{max}}{\sigma^c} = \frac{4}{n}$$

EXAMPLE $n=2$:
$\ell = R/2$

IF A LONGITUDINAL FORCE Q IS PRESSING IN THE DIRECTION OF THE STEM AXIS, IT INDUCES COMPRESSIVE STRESSES. BUT IF IT IS NOT ACTING PRECISELY IN THE MIDDLE OF THE STEM CROSS-SECTION, BUT A LITTLE OFF-CENTRE, I.E. EXCENTRICALLY ON THE LEVER ARM ℓ, THEN IT WILL ALSO INDUCE THE BENDING MOMENT $M = Q \cdot \ell$, AND THUS ALSO PRODUCE BENDING STRESSES. ADDING UP THE COMPRESSIVE AND THE BENDING STRESSES GIVES THE DISTRIBUTION AT THE BOTTOM. WITH $\ell = R/4$ THE TOTAL STRESS ON THE LEFT IS ZERO. THAT IS THE LIMITING VALUE FOR MASONRY COLUMNS. THEY SHOULD NOT UNDERGO ANY TENSILE STRESSES, OR THEY WOULD RUPTURE.

SHEAR AREA: A

FORCE : Q

AVERAGE SHEAR STRESS : $\tau_m = Q/A$

τ_{PAULI}

16

SO THE SHEAR STRESSES ARE CALLED τ (THAT IS THE GREEK LETTER TAU!) AND THEY WERE THE HARDEST FOR PAULI TO COMPREHEND. BUT IT'S STILL QUITE SIMPLE: TWO GLUED PLATES ARE PULLED BY A FORCE Q ALONG THE SHEAR SURFACE A. ACTUALLY THEY WANT TO SLIDE ON EACH OTHER, BUT THE SHEAR STRESSES IN THE GLUELINE WILL PREVENT THIS. THESE EQUAL FORCE/SHEAR SURFACE. NOW THERE IS A MAXIMUM TRANSFERABLE SHEAR STRESS. THIS IS CALLED SHEAR STRENGTH, AND IT IS A CONSTANT OF THE MATERIAL. THE GROUND UNDER PAULI'S PAWS ON A STEEP SLOPE ALSO HAS A SHEAR STRENGTH: τ_{PAULI}. IF PAULI SUPPORTS HIMSELF ON HIS PENCIL, HE WILL INTRODUCE COMPRESSIVE FORCES AND SHEAR FORCES INTO THE GROUND. IF THE SHEAR STRENGTH OF THE GROUND IS EXCEEDED, THEN HIS PAWS WILL SLIDE OFF TO THE LEFT AND HIS PENCIL TO THE RIGHT. THAT'S CALLED SHEAR FAILURE!

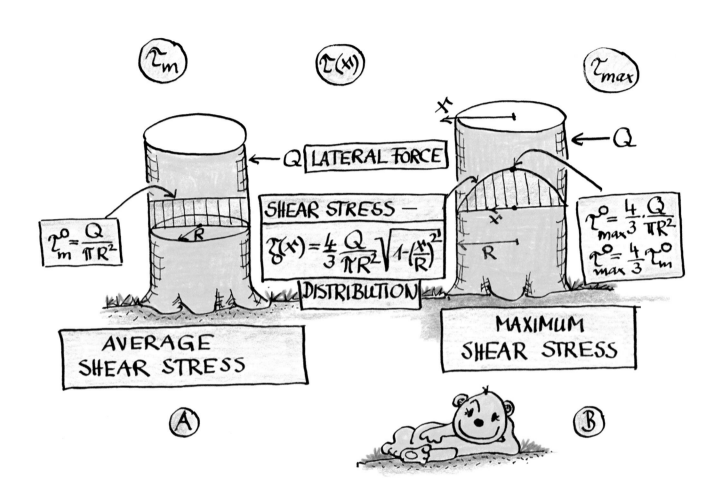

τ_m

$\tau(x)$

τ_{max}

Q LATERAL FORCE

Q

SHEAR STRESS —

$$\tau(x) = \frac{4}{3}\frac{Q}{\pi R^2}\sqrt{1-\left(\frac{x}{R}\right)^2}$$

DISTRIBUTION

$$\tau_m^o = \frac{Q}{\pi R^2}$$

$$\tau_{max}^o = \frac{4}{3}\cdot\frac{Q}{\pi R^2}$$

$$\tau_{max}^o = \frac{4}{3}\,\tau_m^o$$

AVERAGE
SHEAR STRESS

MAXIMUM
SHEAR STRESS

Ⓐ

Ⓑ

18

HERE THE PART OF THE STEM ABOVE THE CIRCLE SHOWN WOULD LIKE TO SLIDE ON THE PART OF THE STEM BENEATH THE CIRCLE. THE SHEAR STRESSES ARE PREVENTING THIS. HERE THE AVERAGED SHEAR STRESSES ARE EQUAL TO THE TRANSVERSE FORCE/SHEAR SURFACE, I.E. STEM CROSS-SECTION (A). BUT WHEN YOU NOTE THAT ON THE SURFACE OF THE TREE'S STEM THE SHEAR STRESSES ARE EQUAL TO ZERO, THEN THE MAXIMUM VALUE IS FOUND IN THE MIDDLE. WITH A CIRCULAR CROSS-SECTION THIS IS 4/3 TIMES GREATER THAN THE MEAN VALUE (B).

AVERAGE

$$\tau_m^o = \frac{Q}{\pi R^2}$$

MAXIMUM

$$\tau_{max}^o = \frac{4}{3}\tau_m^o$$

Ⓐ HORIZONTAL FAILURE

VERTICAL HORIZONTAL SHEAR STRESS

Ⓑ

VERTICAL SHEAR FAILURE

Ⓒ

OF COURSE, IT COULD HAPPEN THAT THE SHEAR STRENGTH OF THE WOOD IS EXCEEDED HERE. THE SHEAR STRESSES IN THE DIRECTION OF THE STEM'S LONGITUDINAL AXIS ARE PRECISELY AS GREAT AS IN THE TRANSVERSE DIRECTION (B). YOU CAN VISUALIZE THIS AS A SMALL ROTATABLE DISC 'NAILED FAST' IN THE TREE, WHICH DOES NOT ROTATE ONLY WHEN THE HORIZONTAL AND VERTICAL SHEAR STRESSES ARE OF EQUAL MAGNITUDE. BUT BECAUSE THE SHEAR STRENGTH IN THE LONGITUDINAL DIRECTION (C) IS MUCH SMALLER THAN TRANSVERSE TO THE STEM (A), LONGITUDINAL SHEAR CRACKS ARE OFTEN OBSERVED, WHERE THE TWO HALVES OF THE TREE ARE SLIDING UPON EACH OTHER. TRANSVERSE FAILURE ACTUALLY OCCURS ONLY WHEN HEDGE-CUTTING WITH THE GARDEN SHEARS, AND EVEN THERE YOU HAVE TO EXERT QUITE A LOT OF PRESSURE, BECAUSE THE SHEAR STRENGTH ACROSS THE GRAIN IS SO HIGH.

LATERAL FAILURE

AXIAL SHEAR = LATERAL SHEAR

AXIAL SHEAR FAILURE

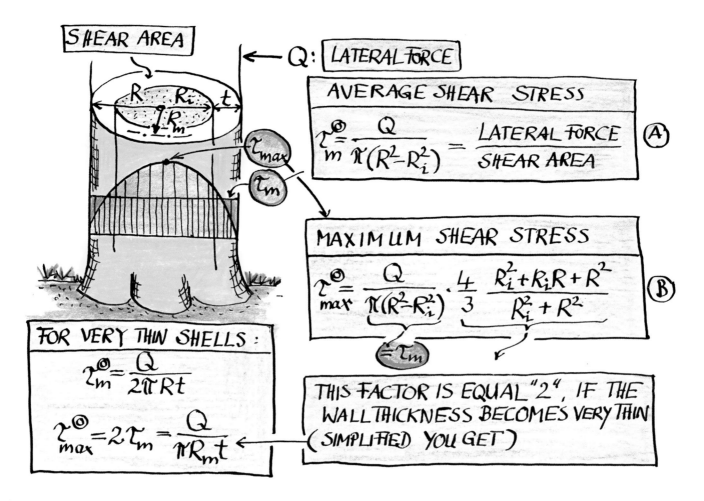

SHEAR AREA

Q: **LATERAL FORCE**

AVERAGE SHEAR STRESS

$$\tau_m^{\varnothing} = \frac{Q}{\pi(R^2 - R_i^2)} = \frac{\text{LATERAL FORCE}}{\text{SHEAR AREA}} \quad \text{(A)}$$

τ_{max}

τ_m

MAXIMUM SHEAR STRESS

$$\tau_{max}^{\varnothing} = \frac{Q}{\pi(R^2 - R_i^2)} \cdot \frac{4}{3} \frac{R_i^2 + R_i R + R^2}{R_i^2 + R^2} \quad \text{(B)}$$

$= \tau_m$

THIS FACTOR IS EQUAL "2", IF THE WALL THICKNESS BECOMES VERY THIN (SIMPLIFIED YOU GET)

FOR VERY THIN SHELLS:

$$\tau_m^{\varnothing} = \frac{Q}{2\pi R t}$$

$$\tau_{max}^{\varnothing} = 2\tau_m = \frac{Q}{\pi R_m t}$$

THE FORMULAE FOR THE SHEAR STRESSES IN HOLLOW TREES ARE A BIT MORE COMPLICATED. HOWEVER, TRANSVERSE-FORCE/SHEAR SURFACE APPLIES HERE TOO FOR THE MEAN VALUE. BECAUSE THE TREE IS HOLLOW, THE AREA OF THE DECAY CAVITY πR_i^2 MUST BE DEDUCTED FROM THE STEM CROSS-SECTION.

BUT IF THE RADIUS R_i OF THE DECAY CAVITY IS PUT AT ZERO, THE CAVITY DISAPPEARS AND YOU AGAIN GET THE OLD FORMULA FOR THE SOLID STEM. JUST TRY THIS.

IF THE THICKNESS OF THE RESIDUAL WALL BECOMES VERY THIN, THEN THE MAXIMUM SHEAR STRESS IS AS MUCH AS 2 TIMES AS HIGH AS THE MEAN. JUST AS IN BENDING, THE PICTURE ON PAGE 22 IS ONLY THE SIDE VIEW OF THE SHEAR-STRESS DISTRIBUTION. BECAUSE THE SHEAR IS ZERO IN THE CAVITY OF THE TREE, THE SPATIAL SHEAR-STRESS DISTRIBUTION IS APPROXIMATELY AS SHOWN HERE.

23

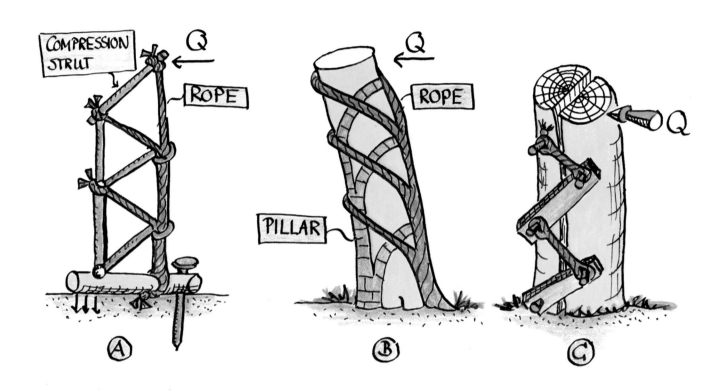

24

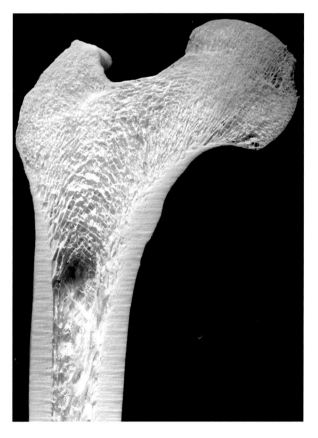

IF THE SHEAR STRESSES DERIVE FROM A TRANSVERSE FORCE, THEN TENSILE AND COMPRESSIVE FORCES WILL ACT AT 45° TO THE DIRECTION OF THE FORCE (A). YOU CAN VISUALIZE THEM AS GUYROPES AND STRUTS. THEREFORE THE PATTERN OF THE TENSILE FORCES AND THE COMPRESSIVE FORCES IN THE TREE IS AS SHOWN IN (B). FINALLY, (C) SHOWS HOW THE 45-DEGREE FORCES PREVENT THE SLIDING OF THE TWO HALVES OF THE TREE, I.E. THE SHEAR CRACK. TENSION- OR COMPRESSION-STRUTS FORMING A FRAMEWORK ARE ALSO FOUND IN THE HUMAN FEMUR. IT IS CURIOUS TOO THAT THERE ARE SO VERY MANY FRAMEWORK STRUTS ONLY WHEN THE BONE IS HOLLOW FOR MORE THAN 70% OF THE RADIUS. THEN THE MICRO-FRAMEWORK STRUTS (CALLED TRABECULAE) STRENGTHEN THE BONE INTERNALLY.

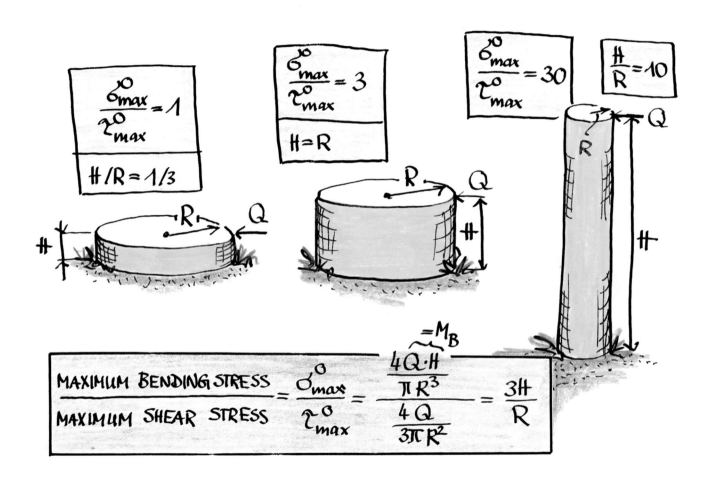

$$\dfrac{\overset{o}{\sigma}_{max}}{\overset{o}{\tau}_{max}} = 1$$

$$H/R \approx 1/3$$

$$\dfrac{\overset{o}{\sigma}_{max}}{\overset{o}{\tau}_{max}} = 3$$

$$H = R$$

$$\dfrac{\overset{o}{\sigma}_{max}}{\overset{o}{\tau}_{max}} = 30$$

$$\dfrac{H}{R} = 10$$

$$\dfrac{\text{MAXIMUM BENDING STRESS}}{\text{MAXIMUM SHEAR STRESS}} = \dfrac{\overset{o}{\sigma}_{max}}{\overset{o}{\tau}_{max}} = \dfrac{\overbrace{\dfrac{4Q \cdot H}{\pi R^3}}^{= M_B}}{\dfrac{4Q}{3\pi R^2}} = \dfrac{3H}{R}$$

26

NOW WHEN A TRANSVERSE FORCE Q IS OPERATING, WHICH IS ACTUALLY GREATER: THE BENDING STRESSES OR THE MAXIMUM SHEAR STRESSES?

THIS DEPENDS ON THE HEIGHT/RADIUS RATIO OF THE STEM. IN THE THICK STUMP ON THE LEFT THE BENDING AND SHEAR STRESSES ARE OF EQUAL MAGNITUDE. IN THE MIDDLE PICTURE THE BENDING STRESSES ARE 3 TIMES GREATER, AND ON THE RIGHT 30 TIMES GREATER THAN THE SHEAR STRESSES. FOR THE SOLID STEM THE BENDING STRESSES ARE GREATER THAN THE SHEAR STRESSES BY A FACTOR OF $(3 \cdot H/R)$. IF DESPITE THIS SHEAR CRACKS OFTEN OCCUR IN TREES BEFORE BENDING FAILURE STARTS, THEN THIS IS DUE TO SMALL SHEAR STRENGTHS IN THE LONGITUDINAL DIRECTION. SHEAR CRACKS OFTEN START AT LARGE RAYS. THAT'S WHY OAKS HAVE SO MANY SHEAR CRACKS, AND MOST IMPORTANT: ROOTS OFTEN CAUSE ADDITIONAL SHEAR STRESSES (SEE PAGE 120), WHICH MAY BE ABOUT 40 TIMES HIGHER COMPARED TO THOSE HIGHER UP IN THE STEM.

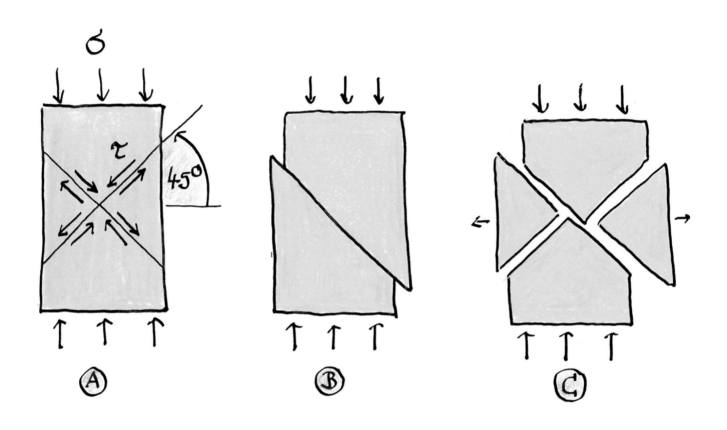

σ

τ

$45°$

Ⓐ   Ⓑ   Ⓒ

28

HOWEVER, THERE ARE ALSO SHEAR STRESSES WHICH ARE HALF AS GREAT AS THE RELEVANT COMPRESSIVE STRESSES. FOR EXAMPLE, IF YOU PRESS ON A STONE OR A BLOCK OF WOOD, IT MAY FAIL AS A RESULT OF SHEAR STRESSES WHICH REACH THEIR HIGHEST VALUE AT AN ANGLE OF 45° MEASURED FROM THE DIRECTION OF COMPRESSION (A,B). STONES MAY FAIL AS IN DRAWING (C). AND WOOD SPECIMENS THAT HAVE FAILED BY SHEAR ARE SHOWN ABOVE. FAILURE CAN BE RECOGNIZED ON THE STEM, ON THE 2-CM BLOCK OF WOOD, AND ON THE MINI-SPECIMEN WHICH IS ONLY A FEW MILLIMETRES IN SIZE. THE FAILURE ANGLE MAY ALSO DEVIATE FROM 45°. THE TREE THEN FORMS BULGE-WOOD ALONG THE SHEAR LINES AND REPAIRS THE SHEAR FAILURE. THESE BULGES APPEAR ON THE TREE ON THE COMPRESSION SIDE OF THE BENDING.

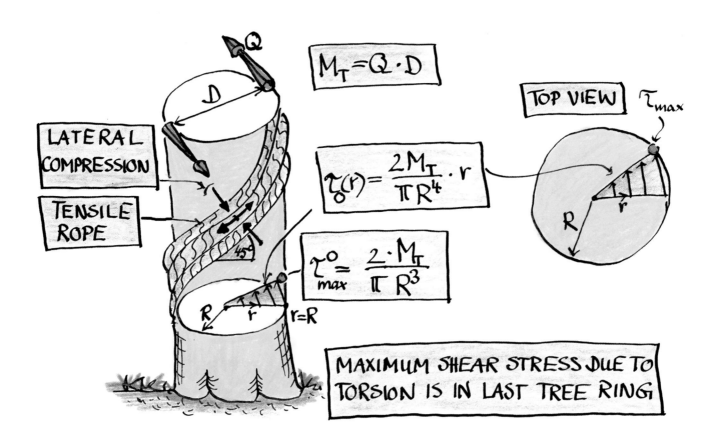

$$M_T = Q \cdot D$$

LATERAL COMPRESSION

TENSILE ROPE

$$\tau_\emptyset(r) = \frac{2 M_T}{\pi R^4} \cdot r$$

$$\tau_{max}^\emptyset = \frac{2 \cdot M_T}{\pi R^3}$$

TOP VIEW

τ_{max}

MAXIMUM SHEAR STRESS DUE TO TORSION IS IN LAST TREE RING

THE TORSION ALSO PRODUCES SHEAR STRESSES IN THE STEM CROSS-SECTION. THESE INCREASE FROM THE INSIDE OUTWARDS. THE TENSILE STRESSES ARE AGAIN TWISTED BY 45° TO THE SHEAR SURFACE, AND COIL THE STEM UPWARDS LIKE ROPES. COMPRESSIVE STRESSES OCCUR PERPENDICULAR TO THE GUYROPES. THEY PRESS THE 'ROPES' TOGETHER TRANSVERSELY.

TREES TWISTED BY THE WIND MAKE THEIR FIBRES INTO GUYROPES. THESE CANNOT KINK, AND NEITHER CAN THEY SPLIT BECAUSE THE TRANSVERSE COMPRESSION IS PRESSING THEM AGAINST EACH OTHER. YOU SHOULD NOT TWIST A SPIRAL-GROWN TREE THE WRONG WAY OR TWIST CRACKS WILL OCCUR. THE TENSILE AND COMPRESSIVE STRESSES ON THE 'ROPES' ARE PRECISELY THE SAME MAGNITUDE AS THE RELEVANT TORSIONAL SHEAR STRESSES.

31

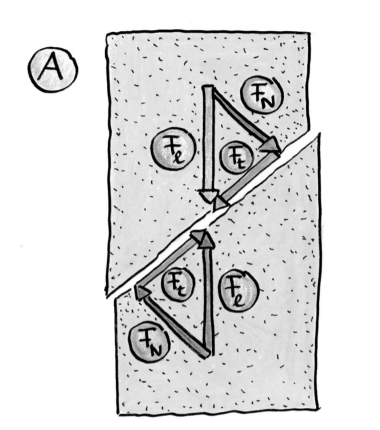

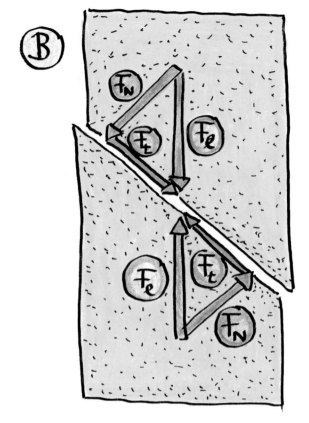

IN THE LAST TWO EXAMPLES SECRET SHEAR STRESSES OCCUR AS WELL AS TENSILE OR COMPRESSIVE STRESSES. WE'LL HAVE A LOOK AT THESE NOW.

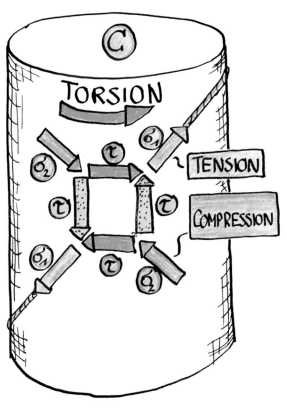

FIGURES A AND B SHOW HOW A LONGITUDINAL FORCE $\overline{F_\ell}$ CAN BE BROKEN DOWN INTO A FORCE $\overline{F_N}$ WHICH IS PERPENDICULAR ON A CHOSEN SLIP LINE AND A TANGENTIAL FORCE $\overline{F_t}$. THE TANGENTIAL FORCES ACTING ON BOTH SIDES OF THE SLIP LINE THEN PRODUCE THE SHEAR STRESSES ALONG THE SLIP LINE. IF THE SLIP LINE IS INCLINED 45° TO THE LONGITUDINAL FORCE, THE GREATEST SHEAR STRESSES WILL ACT THERE. IN THE CASE OF TORSION LOAD (FIGURE C) THE STRESSES ARE ALSO DRAWN IN. HERE TOO THE NORMAL STRESSES σ_1 AND σ_2 ARE DISPLACED BY 45° TO THE SHEAR STRESSES τ. AS YOU SEE, THERE ARE ALWAYS MANY STRESSES ACTING IN A STRUCTURAL COMPONENT, AND IT DEPENDS FROM WHICH DIRECTION YOU CONSIDER IT.

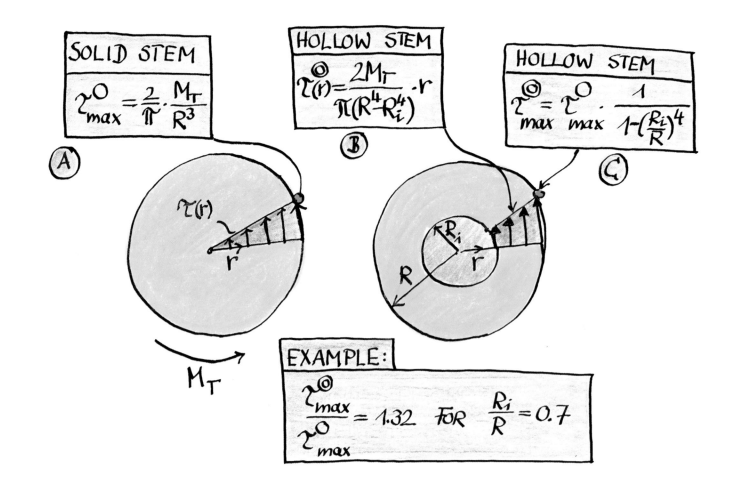

SOLID STEM

$$\mathcal{T}_{max}^{O} = \frac{2}{\pi} \cdot \frac{M_T}{R^3}$$

Ⓐ

HOLLOW STEM

$$\mathcal{T}(r) = \frac{2 M_T}{\pi (R^4 - R_i^4)} \cdot r$$

Ⓑ

HOLLOW STEM

$$\mathcal{T}_{max}^{\odot} = \mathcal{T}_{max}^{O} \cdot \frac{1}{1 - \left(\frac{R_i}{R}\right)^4}$$

Ⓒ

$\mathcal{T}(r)$

r

M_T

R_i

R

r

EXAMPLE:

$$\frac{\mathcal{T}_{max}^{\odot}}{\mathcal{T}_{max}^{O}} = 1.32 \quad \text{FOR} \quad \frac{R_i}{R} = 0.7$$

34

IF SUCH A TWISTED TREE IS MADE INCREASINGLY HOLLOW, THEN THE TORSIONAL SHEAR STRESSES WILL INCREASE ONLY SLOWLY. THEY ARE CERTAINLY SMALLEST IN THE MIDDLE, AND SO IF THE MIDDLE IS MISSING THEN IT DOESN'T MATTER TOO MUCH. IT'S THE SAME AS WITH THE BENDING STRESSES. IF THE STEM IS HOLLOW FOR **70%** OF THE RADIUS ($R_i / R = 0.7$), THEN THE SHEAR STRESSES ARE **1.32** TIMES GREATER THAN IN THE SOLID STEM. JUST LIKE THE BENDING STRESSES ALREADY DISCUSSED ON PAGE **12.** IN CONTRAST, THE SHEAR STRESSES PRODUCED BY A TRANSVERSE FORCE WHEN THE STEM IS HOLLOWED OUT TO $R_i / R = 0.7$ ARE INCREASED **3**-FOLD, BECAUSE THEY ARE GREATEST IN THE MIDDLE. AND IF THIS MIDDLE IS REMOVED, THE REMAINING PART MUST CERTAINLY CARRY MORE LOAD.

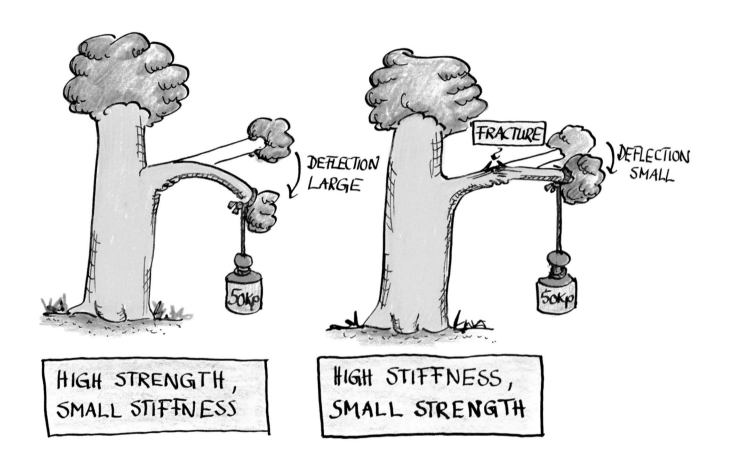

DEFLECTION LARGE

HIGH STRENGTH, SMALL STIFFNESS

FRACTURE

DEFLECTION SMALL

HIGH STIFFNESS, SMALL STRENGTH

A MATERIAL CAN BE DESCRIBED VERY WELL BY ITS STIFFNESS AND STRENGTH, WHICH HAVE NOTHING TO DO WITH EACH OTHER. IF A MATERIAL IS STIFF, IT WILL NOT BE DEFORMED MUCH WHEN LOADED. IN CONTRAST, IF IT IS STRONG, IT WILL NOT BREAK EASILY, NO MATTER HOW MUCH IT IS DEFORMED! IF YOU BEND A BRANCH, YOU DON'T KNOW EXACTLY WHEN IT WILL BREAK.

THE BRANCH ON THE LEFT IS NOT VERY STIFF, IT BENDS A LOT UNDER THE LOAD, BUT IT DOES NOT BREAK. IN CONTRAST, THE BRANCH ON THE RIGHT IS STIFF, IT BENDS ONLY SLIGHTLY, BUT IT BREAKS UNDER THE LOAD.

JUST DRAW A BRANCH WHICH IS STIFF AND STRONG, AND ONE WHICH IS NEITHER STIFF NOR STRONG. IS A RUSK STIFF OR STRONG?

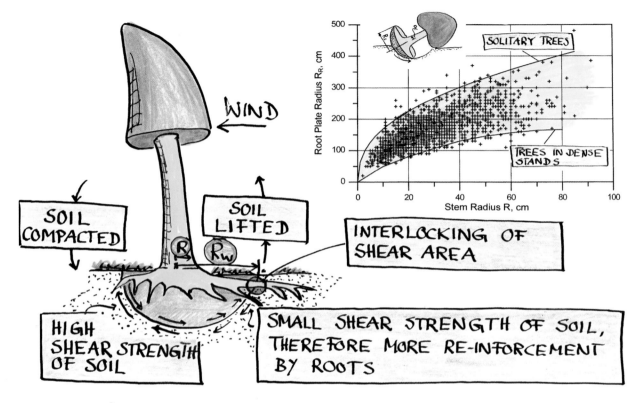

MOHR-COULOMB'S LAW OF SOIL MECHANICS STATES THAT THE SHEAR STRENGTH OF SOIL
INCREASES THE MORE THE SHEAR LOADED SURFACES ARE PRESSED TOGETHER. TREES
PRESS THE SOIL TOGETHER ON THE SIDE AWAY FROM THE WIND (LEE-SIDE), BUT THEY
LIFT THE SOIL UP ON THE WINDWARD SIDE (LUFF-SIDE).

ACCORDINGLY THE ROOTS ARE UNDER GREATER LOAD ON THE WINDWARD SIDE, AND THIS STIMULATES THEM TO MORE GROWTH. THEREFORE THERE ARE MORE, LONGER, THICKER AND PRESUMABLY MORE TENSION-RESISTANT ROOTS ON THE WINDWARD SIDE, IN ORDER TO REINFORCE THE SOIL WHICH IS THERE LESS RESISTANT TO SHEAR. IF THE TREE IS THROWN OVER BY A STORM, THE ROOT-PLATE SHEARS OUT OF THE SOIL. THE WINDTHROW DIAGRAM (ON P. 38) IS BASED ON 2500 WINDTHROWN TREES.

THE UPPER LINE IS FOR SOLITARY TREES AND THE LOWER LINE FOR TREES IN DENSE STANDS. IT SHOWS HOW LARGE IS THE ROOT-PLATE TWISTED OUT FOR ANY GIVEN STEM RADIUS. SO YOU KNOW WHERE TO LOOK FOR SOIL CRACKS WITH A STANDING TREE OF GIVEN STEM RADIUS. WHEN THE SOIL IS VERY WET THE SHEAR STRENGTH OF THE SOIL DECREASES, ESPECIALLY THE COHESION. THIS IS A BONDING OF THE SOIL PARTICLES WHICH IS THERE EVEN WITHOUT CONTACT PRESSURE ON THE SHEAR SURFACES. BASIC SHEAR STRENGTH, SO TO SPEAK!

39

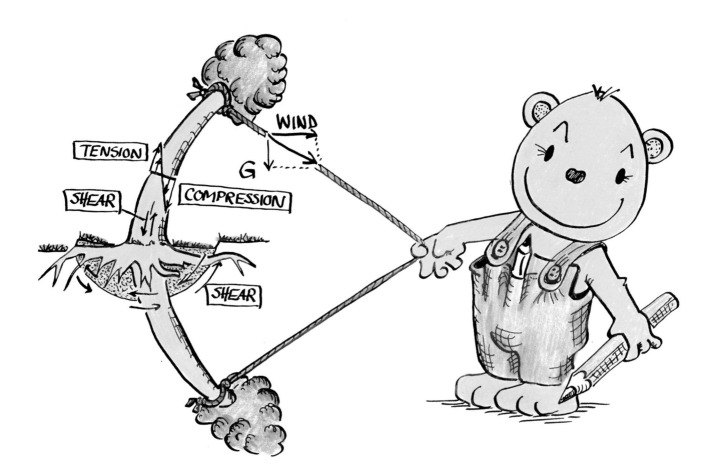

THIS BOW MODEL FOR THE TREE SHOWS US WHAT ENORMOUS FORCES A ROOT-PLATE MUST ABSORB. IF IT DIDN'T EXIST THEN THERE WOULD NEED TO BE A SECOND TREE UNDER THE GROUND, LIKE A MIRROR IMAGE. THE TWO TREES THEN FORM THE ARMS OF AN ARCHER'S BOW. THAT'S WHY YOU SHOULD NEVER CHOP AWAY ANY ROOTS FROM THE TREE. THAT WOULD BE JUST LIKE SAWING INTO THE BOW IN THE MIDDLE. THE RESULT CAN'T BE GOOD! IT IS ESPECIALLY BAD IF THE ROOTS ARE CHOPPED OFF ON THE TENSION SIDE, BECAUSE THE LOOSE SOIL THERE IS NOT SHEAR-RESISTANT AND THE ROOTS HAVE TO 'INTERLOCK' THE SHEAR SURFACE.

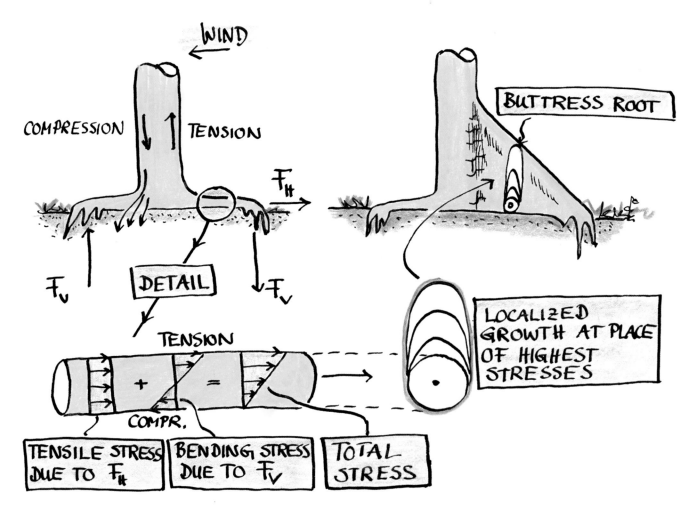

WIND

COMPRESSION

TENSION

F_H

F_V

DETAIL

F_V

BUTTRESS ROOT

TENSION

+

COMPR.

=

TENSILE STRESS DUE TO F_H

BENDING STRESS DUE TO F_V

TOTAL STRESS

LOCALIZED GROWTH AT PLACE OF HIGHEST STRESSES

42

TREES LAY DOWN WOOD WHERE IT IS NEEDED, I.E. WHERE THE MECHANICAL STRESSES ARE HIGH. THIS ALSO EXPLAINS THE FORMATION OF BUTTRESS ROOTS. WHEN THE WIND BENDS A TREE, THEN A COUNTER-FORCE F_H IS NEEDED ON THE ROOT ON THE WINDWARD SIDE, SO THAT THE TREE IS NOT DISPLACED LATERALLY. THIS PRODUCES A UNIFORMLY DISTRIBUTED TENSILE STRESS IN THE ROOT, BUT A VERTICAL FORCE F_V IS ALSO NEEDED TO PREVENT THE TREE FROM TIPPING OVER. THIS FORCE F_V CREATES A BENDING STRESS IN THE ROOT, I.E. TENSILE STRESSES ON TOP AND COMPRESSIVE STRESSES BELOW. THE TWO STRESS DISTRIBUTIONS TOGETHER PRODUCE A MAXIMUM TENSILE STRESS ON THE UPPER SIDE AND THE STRESSES PRACTICALLY CANCEL EACH OTHER OUT BELOW. THUS THE ROOT IS MECHANICALLY STIMULATED TO PRODUCE THICK ANNUAL RINGS ONLY ON TOP. OVER THE YEARS THIS FIRST CAUSES THE WELL-KNOWN LARGE ROOT JUNCTION ON THE WINDWARD SIDE AND LATER A BUTTRESS ROOT MAY DEVELOP FROM IT. ON THE LEE-SIDE IS NO BUTTRESS ROOT BECAUSE THE COMPRESSION FORCE ENTERS THE SOIL CLOSE TO THE STEM AND DOES NOT TRAVEL LONG DISTANCE THROUGH THE ROOT.

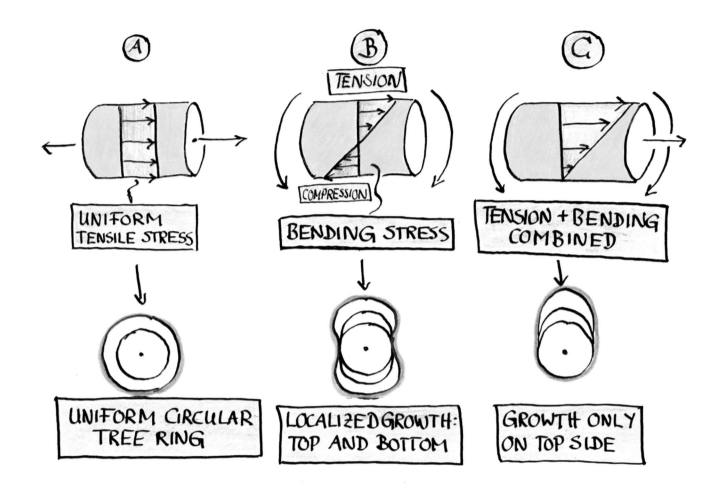

44

IN THIS WAY, THE FOLLOWING ROOT FORMS CAN BE EXPLAINED:

A: UNIFORMLY DISTRIBUTED TENSILE OR COMPRESSIVE STRESSES LEAD TO UNIFORM INCREMENTS, I.E. AN ANNUAL RING THAT IS OF EQUAL THICKNESS ALL THE WAY AROUND.

B: PURE BENDING STRESSES LEAD TO THICK ANNUAL RINGS ON TOP ON THE TENSION SIDE AND ALSO BELOW ON THE COMPRESSION SIDE. THE INCREMENTS ARE VERY SMALL, ALMOST ZERO, IN THE MIDDLE ON THE FIBRES THAT ARE NEUTRAL AS REGARDS BENDING.

C: ADDING THE STRESSES FROM A AND B, WE AGAIN GET THE STRESS DISTRIBUTION ALREADY MENTIONED PREVIOUSLY, WHICH LEADS ONLY TO INCREMENT ON THE UPPER SIDE AND THUS TO BUTTRESS-ROOT FORMATION.

NOTE: ROOTS DO NOT FORM REACTION WOOD, I.E. NEITHER THE COMPRESSION WOOD OF CONIFERS NOR THE TENSION WOOD OF BROADLEAVED TREES, WHICH DOES HOWEVER OCCUR IN BRANCHES. YOU MUST REMEMBER THIS WHEN INTERPRETING BRANCH CROSS-SECTIONS, WHERE EVERYTHING IS MORE DIFFICULT (SEE PAGE 68).

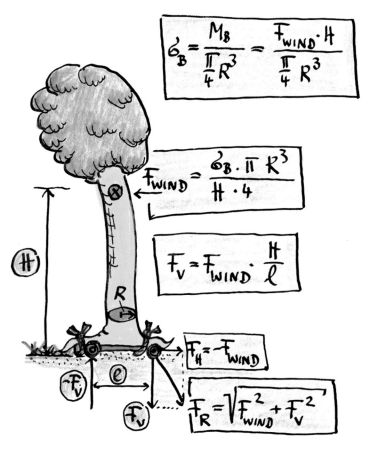

$$\sigma_B = \frac{M_B}{\frac{\pi}{4} R^3} = \frac{F_{WIND} \cdot H}{\frac{\pi}{4} R^3}$$

$$F_{WIND} = \frac{\sigma_B \cdot \pi R^3}{H \cdot 4}$$

$$F_V = F_{WIND} \cdot \frac{H}{\ell}$$

$$F_H = F_{WIND}$$

$$F_R = \sqrt{F_{WIND}^2 + F_V^2}$$

YOU OFTEN NEED TO KNOW HOW GREAT IS THE WIND LOADING AT WHICH A TREE WILL BREAK. THEN THE MAXIMUM BENDING STRESS IS EQUAL TO THE BENDING STRENGTH OF THE WOOD. ASSUMING THAT THE WIND FORCE IS ACTING ON THE CENTRE OF GRAVITY OF THE SURFACE, YOU CAN WORK OUT THE LEVER ARM H. IF YOU CUT OUT THE PICTURE OF A TREE AND PLACE YOUR FINGER UNDER THE CENTRE OF GRAVITY OF THE SURFACE, THEN THE TREE WILL BALANCE ON YOUR FINGER. THUS YOU CAN DETERMINE IT APPROXIMATELY.

IF YOU WANT TO KNOW HOW GREAT THE MAXIMUM ROOT FORCES ARE, BECAUSE THEY ARE THREATENING A PIPELINE IN THE SOIL NEAR BY, YOU MUST CALCULATE THE RESULTANT ANCHOR FORCE F_R. FOR THIS LET US IMAGINE THE TREE AS A WIND VEHICLE. THE HORIZONTAL FORCE F_H IS AS LARGE AS THE WIND FORCE F_{WIND}, BECAUSE THE HORIZONTAL FORCES MUST BE IN EQUILIBRIUM THEMSELVES. THEY PREVENT THE WIND VEHICLE FROM VEERING OFF TO THE LEFT. BUT THE WIND LOAD ALSO PRODUCES A BENDING MOMENT $F_{WIND} \cdot H$ WHICH IS TRYING TO OVERTHROW THE TREE. THAT IS PREVENTED BY A BENDING MOMENT OF THE ROOTS $F_V \cdot \ell$ OF EQUAL MAGNITUDE. THE VERTICAL FORCES F_V ARE MUCH GREATER THAN THE WIND LOAD, BECAUSE THE WIND LEVER H IS MUCH LONGER THAN THE ROOT LEVER ℓ. THE RESULTANT WIND FORCE F_R IS THE MAXIMUM LOADING WHICH CAN BE IMAGINED FOR A PIPELINE. THE ROOT LEVER ℓ CAN BE ESTIMATED WITH THE WINDTHROW DIAGRAM (PAGE **38**). ITS MINIMUM VALUE IS EQUAL TO THE STEM DIAMETER, BUT THAT WOULD GIVE GREATLY INCREASED F_R VALUES. IN PRACTICE, A GOOD VALUE FOR ℓ IS $\ell = 2 \cdot R_R / 3$. HERE R_R IS THE RADIUS OF THE ROOT-PLATE WHICH IS TWISTED OUT OF THE SOIL IN WINDTHROW. THE VALUE OF ℓ SHOULD BE MATCHED TO THE CIRCUMSTANCES OF THE SITE ON THE BASIS OF EXPERIENCE.

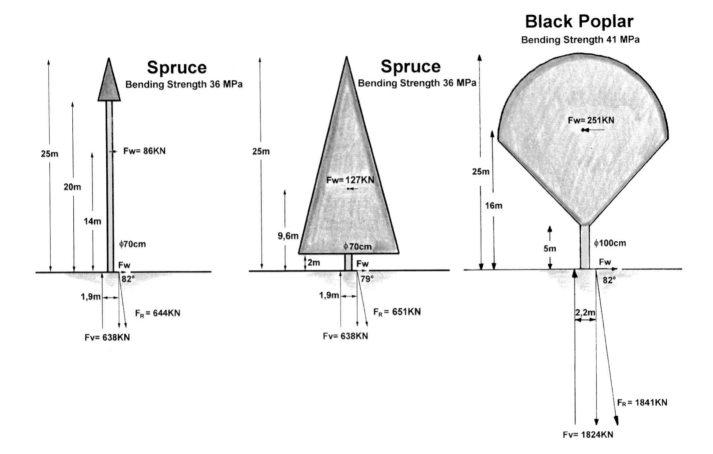

Spruce
Bending Strength 36 MPa

25m
20m
14m
Fw= 86KN
ϕ70cm
Fw
82°
1,9m
F_R = 644KN
Fv= 638KN

Spruce
Bending Strength 36 MPa

25m
9,6m
Fw= 127KN
ϕ70cm
2m
Fw
79°
1,9m
F_R = 651KN
Fv= 638KN

Black Poplar
Bending Strength 41 MPa

Fw= 251KN
25m
16m
5m
ϕ100cm
Fw
82°
2,2m
F_R = 1841KN
Fv= 1824KN

48

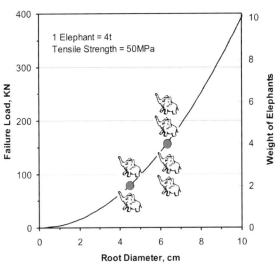

Root Load Capacity

1 Elephant = 4t
Tensile Strength = 50MPa

Failure Load, KN

Weight of Elephants

Root Diameter, cm

THE AXIAL BENDING STRENGTH OF THE WOOD IS NORMALLY TWICE ITS COMPRESSION STRENGTH, WHICH CAN BE MEASURED WITH THE FRACTOMETER II (LAVERS 1983). THE CALCULATED EXAMPLES SHOW THAT SOME POWERFUL ROOT FORCES CAN BE PULLING ON A PIPELINE ON THE WINDWARD SIDE. IF IT IS ASKED WHETHER THESE ARE IN FACT SENSIBLE VALUES, A CHECK CAN BE MADE BY CALCULATING THE ROOT DIAMETERS NEEDED FOR THIS. IT ALL COMES OUT QUITE PLAUSIBLY:

ASSUMING A MINIMUM TENSILE STRENGTH OF 50 MPA = 50N/MM^2 FOR A GUY-ROOT NEAR THE STEM, THEN YOU COULD LIFT TWO ELEPHANTS WITH IT IF IT IS SOMEWHAT MORE THAN 4 CM THICK, AND 10 ELEPHANTS IF IT IS 10 CM THICK. ROOTS AS THICK AS THIS ARE BY NO MEANS RARE. ACCORDINGLY, THE COMPUTED CALCULATIONS CAN BE CHECKED RETROSPECTIVELY FOR PLAUSIBILITY BY OBSERVATIONS IN NATURE.

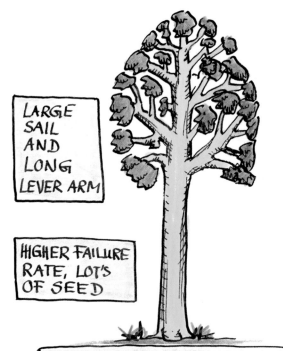

LARGE SAIL AND LONG LEVER ARM

HIGHER FAILURE RATE, LOT'S OF SEED

SMALL SAFETY FACTOR, NATURAL FAILURE RATE EVEN OF HEALTHY TREES, BIG SAIL ABSORBS MUCH LIGHT AND PRODUCES MUCH SEED

$$\text{SAFETY FACTOR} = \frac{\text{FAILURE LOAD}}{\text{SERVICE LOAD}}$$

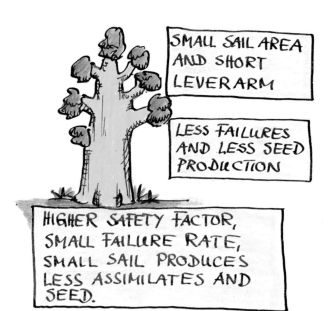

SMALL SAIL AREA AND SHORT LEVER ARM

LESS FAILURES AND LESS SEED PRODUCTION

HIGHER SAFETY FACTOR, SMALL FAILURE RATE, SMALL SAIL PRODUCES LESS ASSIMILATES AND SEED.

THE SAFETY FACTOR S DESCRIBES THE 'MECHANICAL PIGGY-BANK' OF TREES. FOR UNDAMAGED TREES IT IS ABOUT S = 4 TO 4.5. JOHN CURREY AND OTHERS SAY THAT BONES HAVE A SAFETY FACTOR S = 3 TO 4, WITH VERY FEW EXCEPTIONS. IF THE COMPRESSION-LOADED HALF OF A SLIGHTLY LEANING TREE IS SAWN OFF, IT WILL RARELY FALL OVER IMMEDIATELY EVEN THOUGH IT HAS BENDING STRESSES ABOUT 4 TIMES HIGHER. THAT MEANS THAT A HEALTHY TREE CAN BE WEAKENED SO MUCH THAT IT HAS BENDING STRESSES OVER FOUR TIMES HIGHER. THEN ITS RESERVES OF SAFETY ARE USED UP. DO NOT ALLOW TRAFFIC UNDER SUCH A TREE. DESPITE THESE SAFETY RESERVES, EVEN HEALTHY TREES MAY FALL IN A HURRICANE. TREES HAVE A NATURAL FAILURE RATE. NORMALLY NO-ONE IS HELD LIABLE FOR SUCH ACCIDENTS. NATURE COULD HAVE MADE TREES SAFE EVEN AGAINST ANY HURRICANE. HOWEVER, IN EVOLUTION TREES HAVE DEVELOPED WHICH HAVE A 'NATURAL' FAILURE RATE AND THEY COMPENSATE THESE LOSSES WITH A LARGE LIGHTLY CONSTRUCTED CROWN WHICH PRODUCES MANY SEEDS AND THEREFORE NEW TREES. IN NATURE THE SUFFERING OF THE INDIVIDUAL COUNTS FOR NOTHING - ONLY THE PRESERVATION OF THE SPECIES.

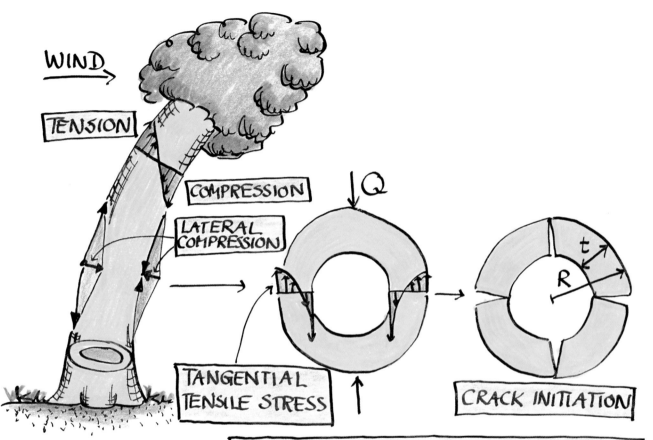

WIND →

TENSION

COMPRESSION

LATERAL COMPRESSION

Q

t

R

TANGENTIAL TENSILE STRESS

CRACK INITIATION

FAILURE INCREASING FOR $t/R \lesssim 0.3$

52

A HOLLOW TREE DOES NOT FAIL PRIMARILY BY BENDING FRACTURE, I.E. BY FIBRE KINKING ON THE COMPRESSION SIDE OF THE BENDING. TRANSVERSE FORCES ARE RESPONSIBLE, WHICH FIRST OVALIZE THE TREE'S CROSS-SECTION AND THEN KINK IT LIKE A HOSEPIPE. THIS USUALLY CAUSES FOUR CRACKS, BUT ONLY THE TWO ON THE NEUTRAL FIBRES OF THE BENDING CAN BE SEEN EXTERNALLY. IN PRACTICE THERE ARE FOUR BENDING POINTS WHERE CRACKS DEVELOP, DISTRIBUTED OVER THE STEM'S CIRCUMFERENCE. IT IS BENDING TENSILE STRESSES IN THE CIRCUMFERENTIAL DIRECTION WHICH INDUCE THE FAILURE (SEE PAGE 124). FIELD STUDIES ON OVER 1600 BROKEN AND STANDING HOLLOW TREES HAVE SHOWN THAT THE FAILURE REALLY STARTS ONLY WHEN THE TREE HAS MORE THAN 65 TO 70% OF THE STEM RADIUS HOLLOW OR ROTTEN. THAT MEANS WHEN THE RATIO OF RESIDUAL WALL THICKNESS/STEM RADIUS, I.E. $t/R \approx 0.3$ APPROXIMATELY OR SMALLER. HOWEVER, THIS PROBABLY APPLIES ONLY FOR FULL-CROWNED TREES. IF THE CROWNS ARE SHORTENED, THE LEVER ARM AND SAIL AREA ARE REDUCED AND THE TREES CAN BE MUCH MORE HOLLOW THAN 70% AND STILL BE SAFE, LIKE AN OLD POLLARD WILLOW FOR EXAMPLE. SO, INDIVIDUAL ASSESSMENT HAS TO BE DONE IN THIS SITUATION.

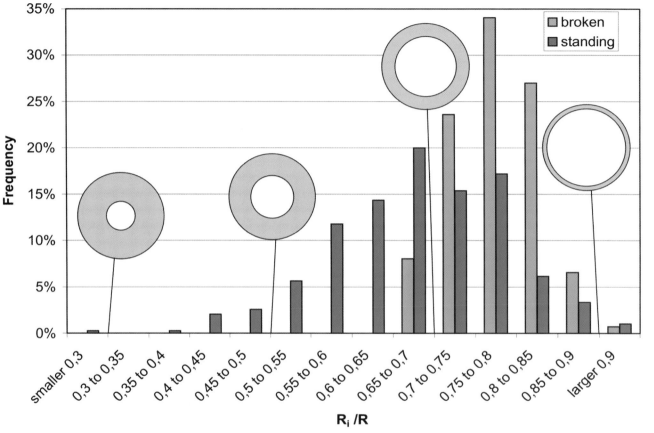

WE HAVE MADE A FIELD STUDY IN THE USA, EUROPE AND AUSTRALIA. THE HISTOGRAM SHOWS THE STANDING HOLLOW TREES AS GREEN AND THE BROKEN HOLLOW TREES AS RED COLUMNS.

54

THE RED COLUMNS BEGIN AT AN INTERNAL-RADIUS/ EXTERNAL-RADIUS RATIO $R_i/R = 0.65 - 0.7$; HOLLOW TREES START TO FAIL AT THIS POINT, BUT YOU DO NOT NEED TO FELL SUCH TREES AT ONCE. THEY CAN BE SHORTENED AND THEN THEY CAN BE SAFE AGAIN. THE MANY GREEN COLUMNS WITH SHORTENED TREES TO THE RIGHT OF $R_i/R = 0.7$ PROVE THIS!

MOREOVER: IN 1985 JOHN CURREY AND MCNEILL ALEXANDER FOUND THAT MOST BONES OF TERRESTRIAL MAMMALS ARE LESS THAN 70% HOLLOW. THE 70% CRITERION THUS SEEMS TO BE FAIRLY GENERALLY VALID.

TREES WITH OPEN CAVITIES PROTECT THEMSELVES AGAINST BUCKLING-IN OF THE 'DOOR-POSTS' BY LAYING DOWN WALLS OF NEARLY DOUBLE THICKNESS THERE, AND MAKING THIS 'DOOR-FRAME' OF ESPECIALLY STRONG WOOD.

Increase of stresses by hollowing

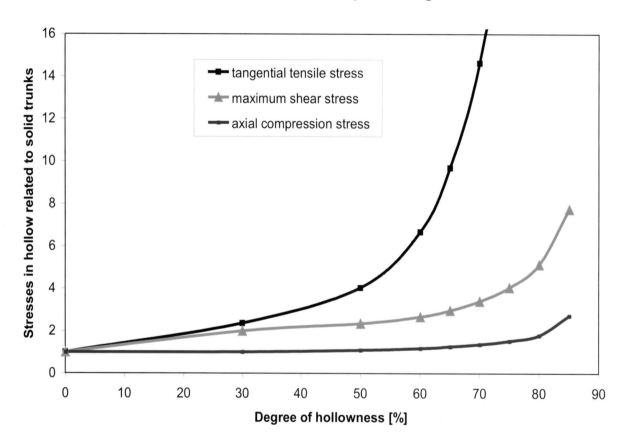

FROM: DOCTORAL THESIS BY MARKUS LEDERMANN, KARLSRUHE, 2002

56

WITH MODERN COMPUTER METHODS (FEM: FINITE ELEMENT METHOD) WE CAN CALCULATE WHAT WILL HAPPEN WITH THE STRESSES IN A HOLLOW TREE STEM WHEN IT IS BENT BY WIND LOADING AND THEN MADE INCREASINGLY HOLLOW. THE TANGENTIAL TENSILE STRESSES INCREASE THE MOST RAPIDLY. THESE ARE STRESSES IN THE DIRECTION OF THE STEM'S CIRCUMFERENCE, I.E. THE ANNUAL RINGS. THEY USUALLY PRODUCE FOUR CRACKS AND INDUCE THE FLATTENING OF THE CROSS-SECTION. NEXT TO INCREASE ARE THE SHEAR STRESSES. HOWEVER, THE BENDING STRESSES IN THE LONGITUDINAL DIRECTION OF THE STEM ARE THE LEAST TO WORRY ABOUT. THEY ARE THE LAST TO INCREASE WITH INCREASING HOLLOWNESS. NATURALLY, NOT ALL TREES HAVE THE SAME STRENGTHS, BUT AGAIN – THE TANGENTIAL TENSILE STRESSES, WHICH INDUCE THE HOSEPIPE KINKING OF THE TREES AND THAT MEANS THE SHATTERING OF THE TREE'S SHELL INTO FOUR BOARD-LIKE SEGMENTS (SEE PAGE 52 AND 124), INCREASE THE MOST RAPIDLY. THE HOLLOW TREE FAILS BY CROSS-SECTIONAL FLATTENING, BY HOSEPIPE KINKING AND ONLY THEN DO THE BOARD-LIKE SEGMENTS FAIL BY BENDING FRACTURE.

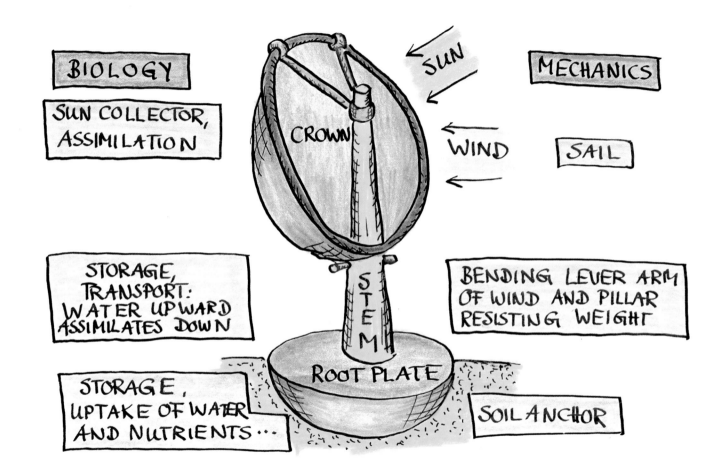

BIOLOGY

MECHANICS

SUN COLLECTOR, ASSIMILATION

SAIL

SUN

WIND

CROWN

STORAGE, TRANSPORT: WATER UPWARD ASSIMILATES DOWN

BENDING LEVER ARM OF WIND AND PILLAR RESISTING WEIGHT

STEM

STORAGE, UPTAKE OF WATER AND NUTRIENTS...

ROOT PLATE

SOIL ANCHOR

ON THE ONE HAND A TREE IS A LIVING THING WHICH CONDUCTS WATER UPWARDS FROM THE ROOTS AND ASSIMILATES DOWNWARDS FROM THE CROWN. THE LONGER THE TRANSPORT PATH, I.E. THE STEM, THE MORE DIFFICULT THIS BECOMES.

ON THE OTHER HAND, THE TREE IS ALSO A SAILING BOAT AND THE LONGER THE BIOLOGICAL TRANSPORT PATH IS, THE LONGER IS THE MECHANICAL LEVER ARM WHICH THE WIND BENDS. BUT WE SHALL SOON SEE THAT THE HEIGHT OF THE TREE STEM, I.E. THE LENGTH OF THE LEVER ARM ALONE, IS NOT A PROBLEM. THE IMPORTANT THING IS HOW THE DIAMETER INCREASES TOWARDS THE BASE, I.E. HOW 'TAPERING' THE TREE IS.

UP THE STEM

DOWN THE STEM

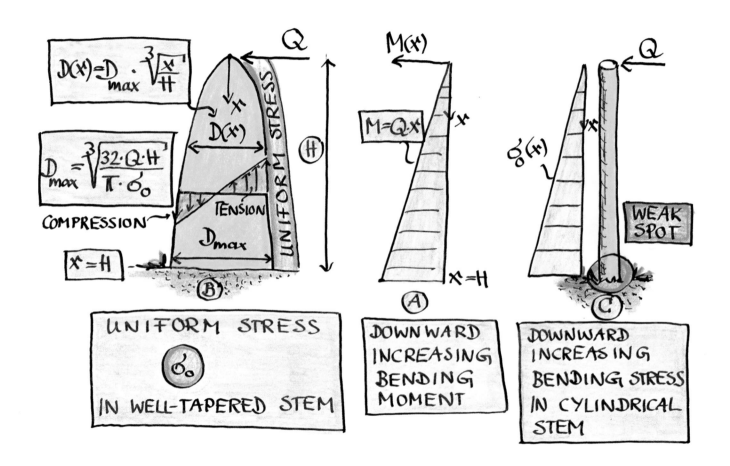

$$D(x) = D_{max} \cdot \sqrt[3]{\frac{x}{H}}$$

$$D_{max} = \sqrt[3]{\frac{32 \cdot Q \cdot H}{\pi \cdot \sigma_o}}$$

COMPRESSION

TENSION

D_{max}

$x = H$

Q

$D(x)$

UNIFORM STRESS

H

(B)

M(x)

$$M = Q \cdot x$$

x

$x = H$

(A)

Q

$\sigma(x)$

x

WEAK SPOT

(C)

UNIFORM STRESS
σ_o
IN WELL-TAPERED STEM

DOWNWARD INCREASING BENDING MOMENT

DOWNWARD INCREASING BENDING STRESS IN CYLINDRICAL STEM

60

IF IT IS REQUIRED THAT THE BENDING STRESSES ALONG THE UPPER SURFACE OF A BEAM ARE CONSTANT, A CONNECTION $D(x)$ IS DERIVED BETWEEN THE DIAMETER D AND THE DISTANCE x FROM THE POINT WHERE THE TRANSVERSE FORCE Q IS ACTING. THE STEM DIAMETER INCREASES DOWNWARDS (FIG. B), BECAUSE THE BENDING MOMENT $M(x)$ (FIG. A) ALSO INCREASES DOWNWARDS.

NOW IF THE TREE IS VERY TALL AND ITS CROWN IS VERY SMALL AND HIGH UP, OFTEN NOT ENOUGH ASSIMILATES GET DOWN. THE TREE SIMPLY DOES NOT HAVE ANY 'CASH' TO FORM A THICK STEM LOW DOWN. IT DOES NOT GROW IN THICKNESS CORRESPONDING TO THE INCREASE IN BENDING MOMENT, AND HAS AN ALMOST CYLINDRICAL STEM (FIG. C). THUS THE STRESSES ARE GREATEST LOW DOWN AND ARE NO LONGER CONSTANT ALONG THE STEM. THE STEM BASE AND ROOT-PLATE ARE THE WEAK PLACE!

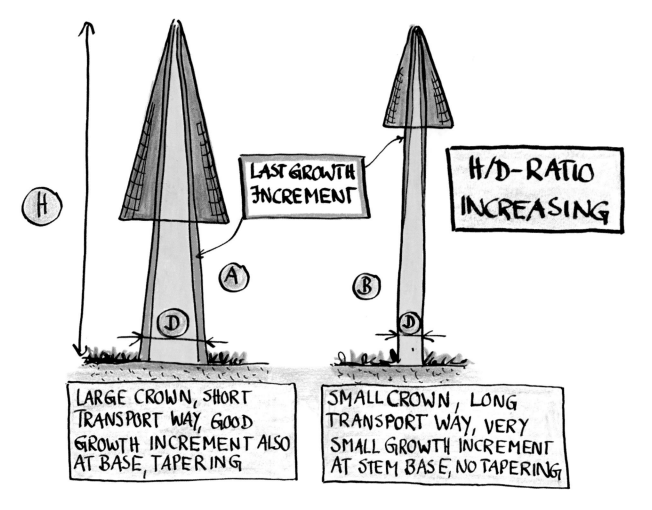

LAST GROWTH INCREMENT

H/D-RATIO INCREASING

LARGE CROWN, SHORT TRANSPORT WAY, GOOD GROWTH INCREMENT ALSO AT BASE, TAPERING

SMALL CROWN, LONG TRANSPORT WAY, VERY SMALL GROWTH INCREMENT AT STEM BASE, NO TAPERING

IN FIG. A THE CROWN IS LARGE ENOUGH AND THE TRANSPORT PATH IS SHORT ENOUGH FOR SUFFICIENT ASSIMILATES TO ARRIVE AT THE BASE. THE STEM BASE AND THE ROOTS PUT ON INCREMENT VIGOROUSLY. THE CONSTANT STRESS DISTRIBUTION CAN BE 'PAID FOR' WITH ABUNDANT ASSIMILATES AND THE TREE IS SAFE IN PRACTICE, BUT IT STILL HAS THE NATURAL FAILURE RATE OF HEALTHY TREES IN A HURRICANE. HOWEVER, IF THE TREE IS VERY TALL AND THE CROWN SMALL, THEN THE ANNUAL RINGS ARE WIDE ONLY AT THE TOP, BUT NARROW DOWN BELOW (FIG. B). THE H/D RATIO BECOMES INCREASINGLY LARGE, AND THE TREE BECOMES INCREASINGLY TOP-HEAVY AND DANGEROUS. THE UNFAVOURABLY HIGH H/D RATIO CAN BE RECOGNIZED, EVEN WITHOUT MEASUREMENT, BY THE FACT THAT THE TREE STEM LOOKS LIKE A CYLINDER AND NOT LIKE A CONE! THE DIAMETER D IS ALWAYS MEASURED ABOVE THE ROOT JUNCTIONS, PREFERABLY AT BREAST HEIGHT.

UP THE STEM

DOWN THE STEM

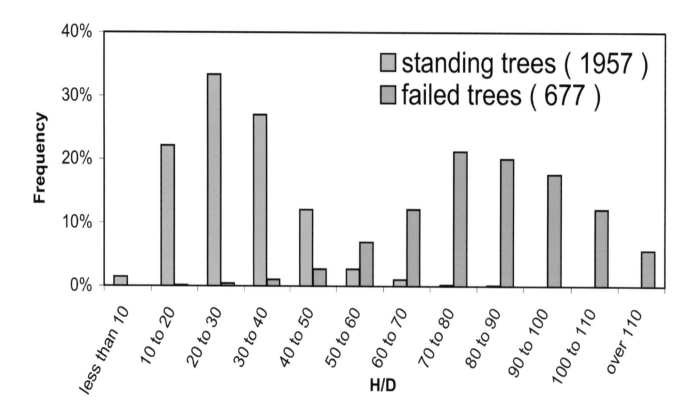

IF THE TREES BECOME INCREASINGLY TOP-HEAVY, THEN AT SOME TIME THEY WILL FALL OVER EVEN IN A MODERATE WIND OR WITH WIND + RAIN LOADING. OUR FIELD STUDIES ON SEVERAL CONTINENTS HAVE SHOWN THAT SOLITARY TREES WITHOUT CLOSE COMPETITORS FOR LIGHT HAVE A FAVOURITE H/D RATIO WHICH LIES BETWEEN H/D = 20 - 35. FAILURE DUE TO A STEM BASE THAT IS TOO THIN STARTS AT ABOUT H/D = 50. THEN THE TREES ARE FIRST BENT BY THE WIND AND THEN FINALLY THE WEIGHT PULLS THEM DOWN. BUT NOTE: HEIGHT ALONE IS NOT A PROBLEM; IT IS THE H/D RATIO THAT COUNTS, I.E. THE TAPER. ANCIENT TALL GIANT SEQUOIAS HAVE A GOOD H/D RATIO OF H/D < 30, BECAUSE THEY ARE SO THICK AT THE BASE. PAULI IS SHOWING HOW TO MEASURE TREE HEIGHT WITH A STICK!

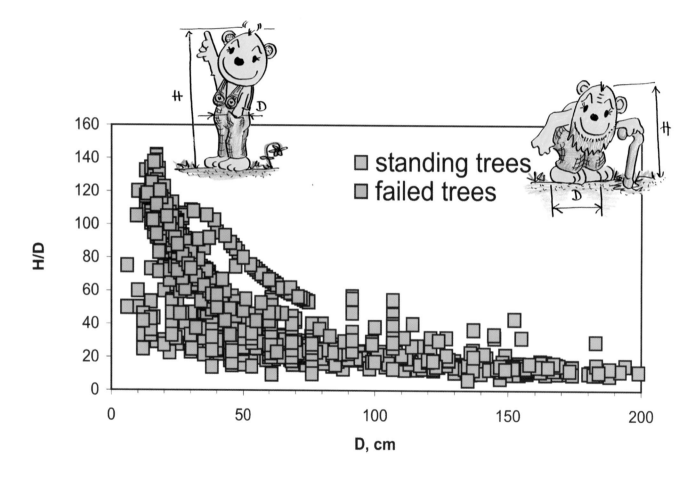

66

THIS SHOWS H/D PLOTTED AGAINST THE STEM DIAMETER MEASURED AT BREAST HEIGHT (DBH) FOR ALL THE TREES EXAMINED.

IN CENTRAL EUROPE THE STEM DIAMETER IS PROPORTIONAL TO THE TREE'S AGE, ACCORDING TO THE MITCHELL FORMULA (TREE AGE = STEM CIRCUMFERENCE (IN CM)/2.5). THIS FORMULA IS BASED ON A MEAN ANNUAL RING WIDTH OF CA. 4 MM. IT IS CLEARLY SEEN THAT THE OLDEST TREES WITH THE LARGEST DIAMETERS HAVE THE SMALLEST H/D RATIO. THOSE WHO LIVE A LONG TIME HAVE A SHORT WIND BENDING LEVER AND SHORT TRANSPORT PATHS. EVEN A YOUNG PAULI IS TALLER AND SLIMMER THAN AN OLD PAULI. WITH THE SIMPLE TOOL SHOWN BELOW YOU CAN MEASURE TREE HEIGHT AND MAKE THE "H/D=50 CHECK".

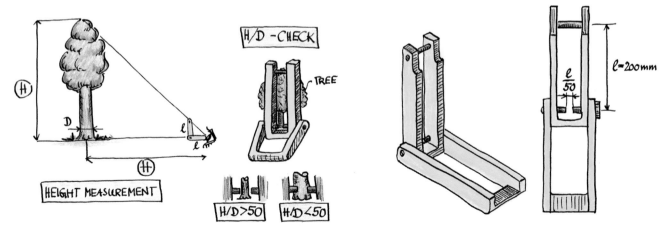

HEIGHT MEASUREMENT

H/D - CHECK

TREE

H/D>50   H/D<50

ℓ=200mm

$\frac{\ell}{50}$

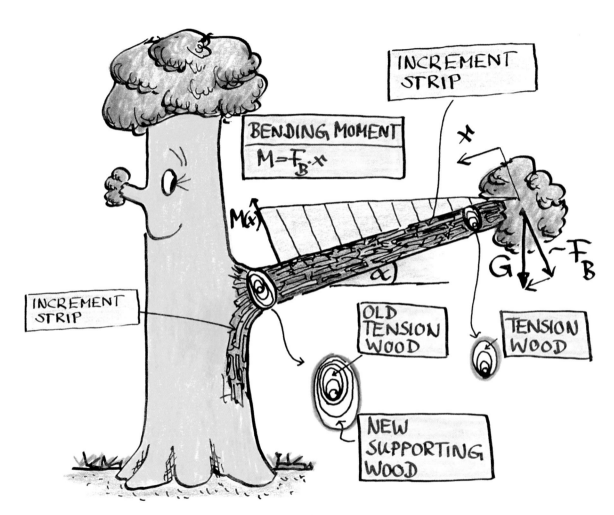

INCREMENT STRIP

BENDING MOMENT
$$M = F_B \cdot x$$

INCREMENT STRIP

$M_{(x)}$

α

OLD TENSION WOOD

TENSION WOOD

NEW SUPPORTING WOOD

G

$\sim F_B$

68

INCLINED BRANCHES CANNOT BE SIMPLY ASSESSED WITH H/D = **50**. IF A LONG BRANCH OF A BROADLEAVED TREE IS NO LONGER FORMING SUFFICIENT TENSION WOOD WHICH HOLDS IT UP LIKE A MUSCLE, THEN ITS UNDERSIDE WILL EXPERIENCE INCREASING COMPRESSION. IT REACTS TO THIS BY FORMING SUPPORTING WOOD. THIS CAN BE CLEARLY RECOGNIZED BY THE INCREMENT STRIPS. AWAY FROM THE STEM, WHERE TENSION WOOD IS STILL BEING FORMED, THEY ARE ON TOP. NEAR THE STEM, WHERE THE FORMATION OF SUPPORTING WOOD IS BEGINNING, THEY ARE UNDERNEATH. THE BENDING MOMENT IS GREATEST NEAR THE STEM AND THERE THE BRANCH CAMBIUM IS ALSO FURTHEST AWAY FROM THE FOLIAGE OF THE BRANCH AND THUS FROM THE PRODUCTION OF ASSIMILATES. IN CONTRAST, THE FORMATION OF TENSION WOOD IS CONTROLLED ONLY BY THE BRANCH ANGLE α. AND THAT IS OF EQUAL MAGNITUDE EVERYWHERE IN OUR EXAMPLE. THE SUMMER DROP OF GREEN BRANCHES OFTEN OCCURS AT THE TRANSITION FROM TENSION WOOD TO SUPPORTING WOOD.

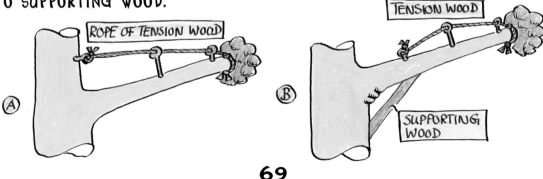

69

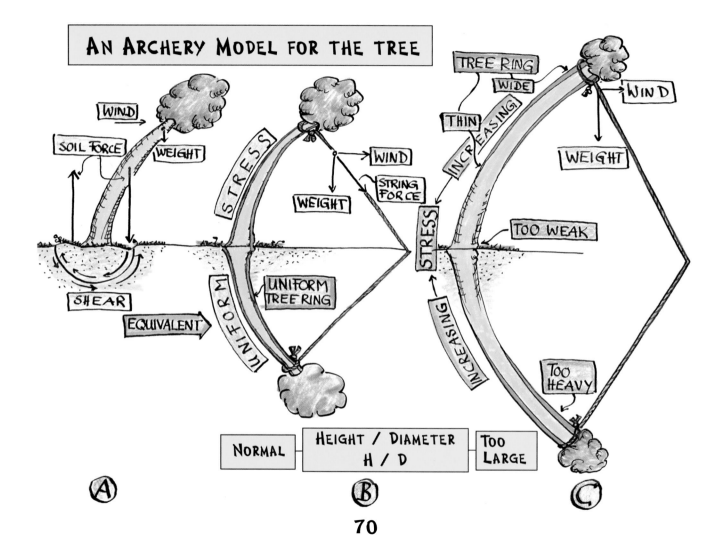

70

ON PAGE 40 WE'VE ALREADY SEEN THAT THE ROOT-PLATE IN FIG. A IS AN INCREDIBLE ACHIEVEMENT OF NATURE, BECAUSE A SECOND UNDERGROUND TREE WOULD ACTUALLY BE NEEDED (FIG. B), WHICH THE ROOT-PLATE REPLACES AS ITS MECHANICAL EQUIVALENT. NOW THE LACK OF TAPER OF THE TREES (I.E. THE EXCESSIVE H/D VALUES) CAN BE EXPLAINED IN THIS BOW MODEL (FIG. C). THE MIDDLE OF THE BOW IS WEAKENED, BUT THAT IS WHERE THE HIGHEST BENDING MOMENTS OCCUR. NO BOW-MAKER WOULD PRODUCE SUCH A NONSENSE.

TRANSPORT WAY, LEVER ARM

LONGER LEVER ARM + WAY

SHORTER LEVER ARM + TRANSPORT WAY

NEW GROWTH

A — NO PRUNING

B — CUTTING OFF LOWER BRANCHES

C — SHORTENING, NO TOPPING, NEW GROWTH BELOW OLD CROWN

72

HERE WE SEE THE TRIMMING MEASURES ON TREES, AND HOW THEY AFFECT THE TREES. THE UNTREATED TREE (A) HAS A UNIFORM INCREMENT. NOW IF THE LOWER BRANCHES ARE SAWN OFF (B) AND THUS THE TRANSPORT PATHS FOR WATER AND ASSIMILATES ARE LENGTHENED, THE ANNUAL RINGS DOWN AT THE STEM BASE ARE MUCH NARROWER. ALSO THE SUPPLY TO THE ROOTS IS MUCH POORER. THE TREE IS GROWING INTO H/D RATIOS THAT ARE TOO HIGH. IT IS BETTER TO SHORTEN THE TREE FROM ABOVE DOWNWARDS (C), BUT ONLY IF THERE ARE REASONS FOR DOING SO, E.G. IF THE STEM BASE OR ROOTS CONTAIN WOOD DECAYS, IF ROOTS HAVE BEEN CHOPPED OFF OR IF THE CROWN HAS A DEAD TOP. WHEN THE CROWN PRODUCES NEW GROWTH DOWN BELOW AFTER THE SHORTENING, THE WHOLE CROWN IS DISPLACED DOWNWARDS. YOU CAN PUT IT LIKE THIS: CUTTING OFF THE LOWER BRANCHES CREATES LONG TRANSPORT PATHS AND BENDING LEVERS, WHEREAS SHORTENING THE CROWN REDUCES BOTH OF THEM ADVANTAGEOUSLY. SHORTENING THE CROWN DOES NOT MEAN TOPPING!!

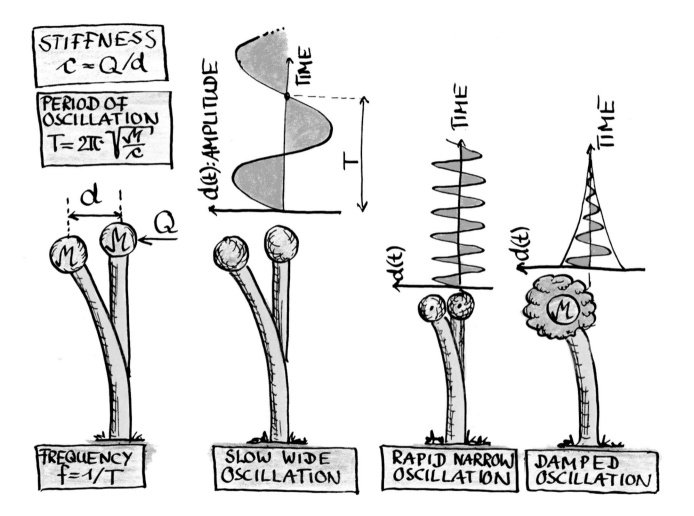

STIFFNESS
$c \approx Q/d$

PERIOD OF OSCILLATION
$T = 2\pi \cdot \sqrt{\dfrac{M}{c}}$

d

Q

$d(t)$: AMPLITUDE

TIME

T

FREQUENCY
$f = 1/T$

SLOW WIDE OSCILLATION

$d(t)$

TIME

RAPID NARROW OSCILLATION

$d(t)$

TIME

DAMPED OSCILLATION

74

THE SLENDER TREES OSCILLATE MORE SLOWLY AND ALSO SWAY OUT FURTHER WITH A GIVEN WIND STIMULUS. THEIR AMPLITUDE OF OSCILLATION IS GREATER. THIS CAN BE SHOWN, GREATLY SIMPLIFIED, ON A BENDING BEAM HAVING NO MASS, ON THE END OF WHICH AN INDIVIDUAL MASS M IS ATTACHED. FIRST THE STIFFNESS c IS CALCULATED. THIS DETERMINES HOW GREAT IS THE SWAY d BY WHICH THE BEAM WILL BEND LATERALLY IF A TRANSVERSE FORCE Q IS ACTING ON IT. FROM THIS THE DURATION OF OSCILLATION T CAN BE CALCULATED FOR ONE PERIOD. THE FREQUENCY f IS EQUAL TO $1/T$. THE EXAMPLES SHOW THAT THE TALL SLENDER TREE HAS GREATER AMPLITUDES $d(t)$ AND THEREFORE ALSO SWAYS MORE SLOWLY. HERE THE WIND WOULD HAVE PLENTY OF TIME FOR A SECOND GUST. THE RISK OF RESONANCE STIMULATION IS GREATER THAN IN A SHORT TREE WHICH SWAYS TO AND FRO RAPIDLY AND EXHIBITS SMALL AMPLITUDES WITH SMALL PERIOD OF OSCILLATION. NOTE ALSO THE DAMPING BY AIR FRICTION – THE AMPLITUDES USUALLY DECREASE QUICKLY.

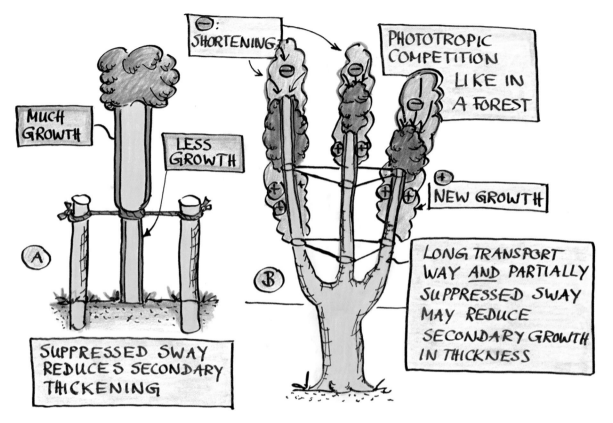

BACK IN 1939 THE AUSTRALIAN JACOBS (PAULI'S FRIENDS IN AUSTRALIA ARE CALLED KOALA BEARS!) SHOWED THAT TREES WHOSE OSCILLATIONS ARE SUPPRESSED BY CABLING MAY PUT ON LESS DIAMETER GROWTH.

WIND

HE REALLY BELIEVES THIS LITTLE ROOT PLATE IS ENOUGH...

THE SAME APPLIES, THOUGH TO DIFFERENT EXTENT, FOR ANY MECHANICALLY EFFECTIVE CABLING IN THE TREE, APART FROM CATCH CABLES WHICH HANG LOOSE, ACCEPT THE BREAKAGE, AND MERELY PREVENT THE ACCIDENT. THEREFORE, PAULI THINKS THAT SHORTENING THE CROWN TAKES PRECEDENCE OVER CABLING. IN ANY CASE THE CABLING (WHICH SHOULD IF POSSIBLE BE A RING-CABLING SYSTEM) SHOULD ALSO BE COMPLEMENTED BY CROWN SHORTENING. THIS WILL ALSO COMPENSATE FOR THE STIFFER SWAYING BEHAVIOUR OF THE CROWN WHICH CABLING MAY CAUSE, AND REDUCE THE POSSIBLE RISK OF WINDTHROW! THE TREE IS ALSO STIMULATED TO NEW GROWTH IN THE LOWER CROWN REGION, AND THUS THE BIOLOGICAL TRANSPORT PATH IS SHORTENED. THIS APPLIES FOR TREES WHICH FORM NEW BRANCHES WHEN THEY ARE SHORTENED.

77

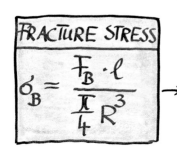

FRACTURE STRESS

$$\sigma_B = \frac{F_B \cdot \ell}{\frac{\pi}{4} R^3}$$

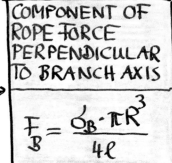

COMPONENT OF ROPE FORCE PERPENDICULAR TO BRANCH AXIS

$$F_B = \frac{\sigma_B \cdot \pi R^3}{4\ell}$$

F_B : BENDING PART OF ROPE FORCE

σ_B : FRACTURE STRESS OF BRANCH WOOD

ℓ : LEVER ARM

78

IF A BRANCH IS SECURED, THEN THE CABLE MUST REPLACE THE FRACTURE MOMENT, $M_B = F_B \cdot \ell$ OF THE BRANCH AT ITS POINT OF ATTACHMENT. THAT MEANS THAT IF THE CABLE IS PULLED IT MUST BE STRONG ENOUGH TO BREAK THE HEALTHY BRANCH CLOSE TO THE STEM. THE NECESSARY BEARING LOAD OF THE CABLE F_S CAN BE CALCULATED IN THIS WAY. ITS BENDING PORTION IS F_B AND ONLY THIS ACTS AGAINST THE DOWNWARDS BENDING OF THE BRANCH. F_D ONLY PRESSES THE BRANCH TOGETHER IN THE LONGITUDINAL DIRECTION. IT IS BEST IF $F_S = F_B$ AND $F_D = 0$. THEN THE CABLE IS AT RIGHT ANGLES TO THE BRANCH. EVEN GOOD CABLING IS NO GUARANTEE OF SAFETY BUT, LIKE A TREE PROP, IT CAN HELP TO WITHSTAND THE EXTERNAL LOADS BETTER. CATCH CABLE FORCES HAVE TO BE DIMENSIONED IN A DIFFERENT WAY, BECAUSE IN THIS CASE INERTIA FORCES AND FALL HEIGHT ARE IMPORTANT.

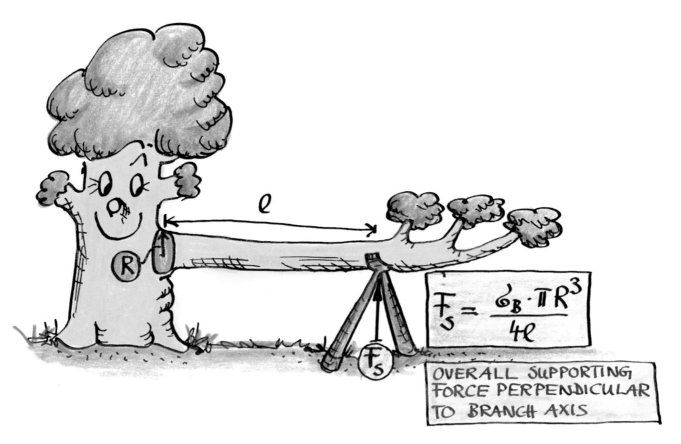

$$F_S = \frac{\sigma_B \cdot \pi R^3}{4\ell}$$

OVERALL SUPPORTING FORCE PERPENDICULAR TO BRANCH AXIS

A TREE SUPPORT CAN BE DIMENSIONED IN EXACTLY THE SAME WAY. USUALLY AN A-FRAME SUPPORT IS CHOSEN WHICH WILL ALSO CATCH THE LATERAL OSCILLATIONS CAUSED BY THE WIND.

IT MUST BE STRONG ENOUGH TO BREAK THE SUPPORTED BRANCH BY BENDING WITH THE LOAD IT CAN SUPPORT, IF UPWARDS PRESSURE IS APPLIED AT ITS FOUNDATIONS. THE MATERIAL OF THE SUPPORT SHOULD NEITHER FAIL LOCALLY NOR KINK! THE TOTAL LOAD OF THE SUPPORT, WHICH IS COMPOSED OF THE TWO ELEMENTS OF THE A-FRAME, IS CALCULATED WITH THE FORMULA FOR F_s. THIS FORMULA CONTAINS THE FRACTURE STRESS OF THE BRANCH WOOD. $\sigma_{\!B}$ IS THE BENDING STRENGTH OF THE WOOD PARALLEL TO THE GRAIN. IT IS ABOUT TWICE AS GREAT AS THE COMPRESSION STRENGTH, WHICH CAN BE MEASURED INDIVIDUALLY WITH THE FRACTOMETER II ON AN INCREMENT CORE, OR CAN BE READ OFF FROM TABLES. HOWEVER, THE TABLES ONLY GIVE MEAN VALUES. THEY ARE PRESENTED ON THE FOLLOWING PAGES.

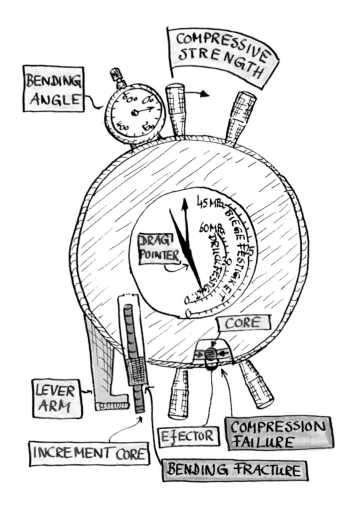

BENDING ANGLE

COMPRESSIVE STRENGTH

DRAG POINTER

45 MPa · BIEGE FESTIGKEIT

60 MPa · DRUCKFESTIGKEIT

CORE

LEVER ARM

EJECTOR

COMPRESSION FAILURE

INCREMENT CORE

BENDING FRACTURE

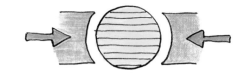

AXIAL COMPRESSIVE STRENGTH

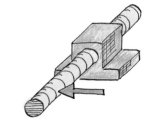

RADIAL BENDING STRENGTH

82

RADIAL BENDING STRENGTH

THE INDIVIDUAL FRACTURE LOAD OF THE TREE OR BRANCH CAN BE DETERMINED MORE ACCURATELY IF INDIVIDUAL STRENGTHS ARE MEASURED. FOR THIS THE FRACTOMETER II IS A WONDERFUL INSTRUMENT IN ITS PURELY MECHANICAL DESIGN. IT MEASURES THE RADIAL BENDING STRENGTH, WHICH IS DETERMINED BY THE RAYS, ON AN INCREMENT CORE $\phi 5mm$ IN DIAMETER. THE AXIAL COMPRESSIVE STRENGTH CAN ALSO BE MEASURED BY LATERAL CRUSHING OF THE CORE, AND APPROXIMATELY TWICE IT'S VALUE IS THE BENDING STRENGTH NEEDED FOR CALCULATING THE DIMENSIONS OF CROWN SECURING CABLES AND A-FRAME SUPPORTS. THE FRACTOMETER II IS ALSO A PORTABLE STRENGTH-TESTING LABORATORY FOR ANYONE WANTING TO INVESTIGATE WOOD. THE WOOD SAMPLES 5MM IN DIAMETER CAN BE TAKEN WITH A HOLLOW STEEL BORER CALLED AN INCREMENT BORER.

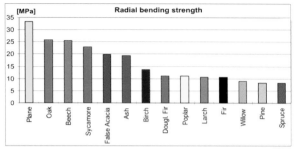

Radial bending strength

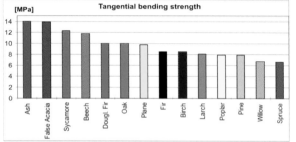

Tangential bending strength

STRENGTHS OF GREEN EUROPEAN
TIMBERS AFTER GÖTZ, 2000

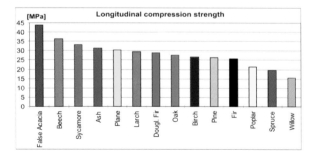

Longitudinal compression strength

84

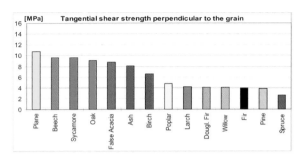

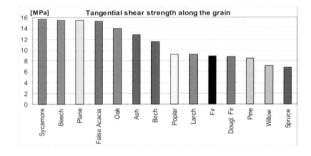

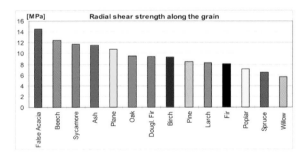

85

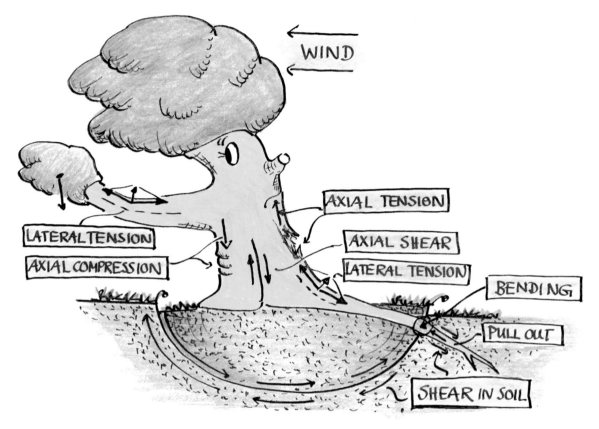

WIND

AXIAL TENSION

LATERAL TENSION

AXIAL COMPRESSION

AXIAL SHEAR

LATERAL TENSION

BENDING

PULL OUT

SHEAR IN SOIL

THE FAILURE OF ANY STRUCTURAL ELEMENT IS ALWAYS THE CULMINATION OF A CONTEST BETWEEN THE INDIVIDUAL STRESSES WHICH, WITH INCREASING EXTERNAL LOADING (STORM, SNOW, OWN WEIGHT, ETC.), ALL RUN TOWARDS THEIR CRITICAL FRACTURE VALUE.

THE STRESS THAT IS THE FIRST TO REACH ITS CRITICAL VALUE, AT WHICH FAILURE OCCURS, WILL DESTROY THE STRUCTURAL ELEMENT. SOME INTERNAL STRESSES ARE SHOWN IN OUR STORM-LASHED TREE: TRANSVERSE TENSILE STRESSES CAN CREATE A SO-CALLED HAZARD-BEAM CRACK IN A BRANCH OR ROOT JUNCTION. THE LONGITUDINAL COMPRESSIVE STRESSES CAN BUCKLE FIBRES, AND THE LONGITUDINAL TENSILE STRESSES CAN RUPTURE THEM. IN THE MIDDLE OF THE STEM, LONGITUDINAL SHEAR STRESSES CAN CREATE A SHEAR CRACK, AND THE SHEAR STRESSES AT THE MARGIN OF THE ROOT-PLATE CAN INDUCE WINDTHROW IF THE SHEAR STRENGTH OF THE SOIL IS EXCEEDED. THEN THE HOLDING ROOT ON THE WINDWARD SIDE MAY BE EITHER TORN OUT OF THE SOIL OR SUFFER A BENDING FRACTURE. THAT IS THE CONTEST OF THE STRESSES. THE VICTOR IS THE FIRST TO REACH THE RELEVANT STRENGTH OF THE MATERIAL AND INDUCE FAILURE. OTHER STRESSES MAY INCREASE OR DECREASE IN CONJUNCTION WITH THIS. COMBINED FAILURE MAY ALSO OCCUR, E.G. HAZARD-BEAM CRACK IN THE ROOT JUNCTION CAUSED BY TRANSVERSE TENSILE STRESSES, WITH SUBSEQUENT WINDTHROW BY EXCEEDING THE SHEAR STRENGTH OF THE SOIL AND BENDING FRACTURE OR TEAR-OUT OF THE HOLDING ROOT AT THE ROOT-PLATE MARGIN WHEN THE GIANT TREE CRASHES DOWN.

SUMMARY OF TREE FAILURE

1. ALL TREES CAN FAIL, EVEN HEALTHY ONES. NO UNTRIMMED TREE IS 100% SAFE.

2. HOLLOW UNTRIMMED TREES HAVE A HIGHER FAILURE RATE IF THEY ARE HOLLOW TO APPROXIMATELY 70% OR MORE OF THEIR RADIUS.

3. TREES WITHOUT DECAY HAVE A HIGHER FAILURE RATE IF THEIR HEIGHT/DIAMETER RATIO IS GREATER THAN H/D = 50 AND THEY ARE FREE-STANDING.

4. EVEN IF JUST ONE ROOT WITH A LARGE JUNCTION IS CHOPPED OFF OR DECAYS, THEN THE OTHERWISE HEALTHY TREE IS NO LONGER SAFE AND MUST BE SHORTENED. THE LARGEST ROOT JUNCTION IS USUALLY ON THE WINDWARD SIDE OR GENERALLY ON THE TENSION SIDE OF THE BENDING.

5. THE REDUCTION OF THE GROWTH STRESSES, ESPECIALLY OF THE TENSION WOOD IN BROADLEAVED TREES, CAN ALSO LEAD TO THE FAILURE OF BRANCHES AND LEANING TREES.

6. EVEN TREES NOT DAMAGED BY DECAY MAY FAIL IF THE SURROUNDING SOIL CANNOT TAKE THE LOADING IMPOSED BY THE TREE. EXAMPLES:
   - STAGNANT WETNESS REDUCES THE SHEAR STRENGTH OF THE SOIL.
   - A THIN SOIL COVER OVER ROCK REDUCES THE ROOT DEPTH AND INCREASES THE RISK.
   - BUILDING WORK MAY PREVENT THE ROOT SYSTEM MATCHING THE LOAD.

7. BUT EVEN COMPLETELY HEALTHY TREES, ROOTED IN THE BEST SOIL, MAY FAIL IN A HURRICANE. EVOLUTION HAS CREATED TREES WHICH HAVE A NATURAL FAILURE RATE. IT IS BETTER TO SEND INTO COMPETITION AN ENERGY-SAVING SPECIES WITH LESS MATERIAL AND THUS TO SACRIFICE INDIVIDUALS IN THE HURRICANE, THAN TO CREATE A VERY HEAVY AND 'EXPENSIVE' SPECIES WITH INDIVIDUALS WHICH WOULD BE SAFE IN ANY HURRICANE, EVEN THOUGH THEY MAY NEVER EXPERIENCE ONE. THIS FAILURE HAS LONG BEEN CLASSED AS ACT OF GOD. BUT IF THE FREQUENCY OF HURRICANES WERE TO INCREASE IN FUTURE, THEN THE QUESTION COULD ARISE OF ARTIFICIALLY INCREASING THE SAFETY FACTOR OF EVEN HEALTHY TREES BY PREVENTIVE CROWN SHORTENING.

THE BODY LANGUAGE
OF
FUNGUS FRUIT BODIES

HAS A LOT TO DO WITH MECHANICS. FUNGI TELL US HOW MUCH WOOD THEY HAVE ALREADY DESTROYED, AND HOW MUCH THE STRENGTH OR STIFFNESS OF THE WOOD HAVE BEEN REDUCED. ALSO, THEY OFTEN INDICATE HOW THE DECAY IS DISTRIBUTED IN THE TREE. THEY ALSO OFTEN TESTIFY WHETHER AN ACCIDENT WAS PREDICTABLE. THIS COULD ALMOST BE CALLED 'FORENSIC MYCOLOGY'!

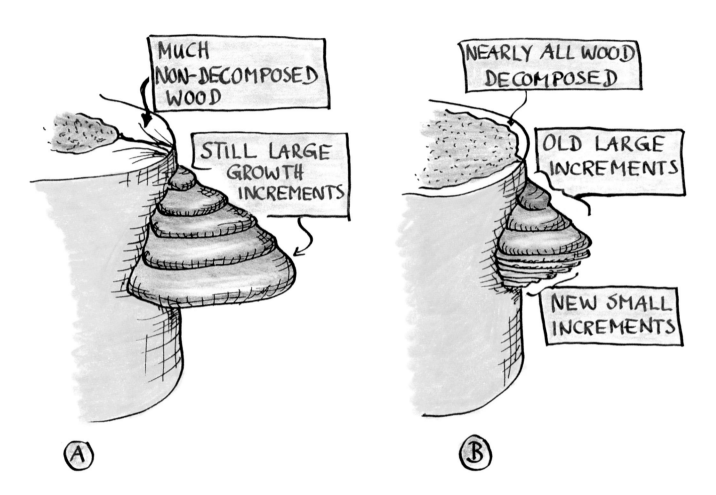

BY THEIR BODY LANGUAGE THE PERENNIAL FRUIT BODIES OF FUNGI TELL US HOW MUCH UNDECAYED WOOD IS STILL TO BE FOUND NEAR THEM IN THE TREE.

IF THE FUNGUS FRUIT BODY IS STILL GROWING STRONGLY, THEN IT STILL HAS ENOUGH WOOD (A). IF THE INCREMENTS ARE DECREASING MORE AND MORE, THEN IT IS RUNNING OUT OF ACCESSIBLE WOOD (B). THE TREE IS ALMOST COMPLETELY DECAYED THERE. IN CASE B THE SIZE OF THE FRUIT BODY IS NOT IMPORTANT - ONLY THE LAST FEW INCREMENTS MATTER. PAULI HAD ALSO HAD A LOT TO EAT, AND NOW HE'S ONLY GOT A BONE LEFT - THAT'S IT.

NOTE: EVEN IN CASE A THE TREE MAY FAIL. ENOUGH WOOD TO FEED FUNGUS DOES NOT NECESSARILY MEAN ENOUGH WOOD FOR A SAFE TREE.

Ⓐ　　　　　Ⓑ

HOWEVER, IT MAY BE THAT EVEN WITH A SIGNIFICANTLY DECLINING FRUIT BODY, THE PART WHERE THE FUNGUS IS ATTACHED IS NOT DECAYED OR ONLY RECENTLY. IT MAY ALSO BE THAT THE WOOD THERE IS HIGHLY REINFORCED WITH FUNGUS TISSUE. YOU CAN'T STICK A HUNTING KNIFE INTO THE PLACE WHERE IT HAS GROWN, EVEN THOUGH THE KNIFE WILL GO IN EVERYWHERE ELSE. THE FUNGUS IS LIKE A PAINTING WHICH IS BREAKING UP THE WALL ON WHICH IT IS HANGING. HOWEVER, IT SAVES THE NAIL AND ITS IMMEDIATE VICINITY UNTIL THE END.

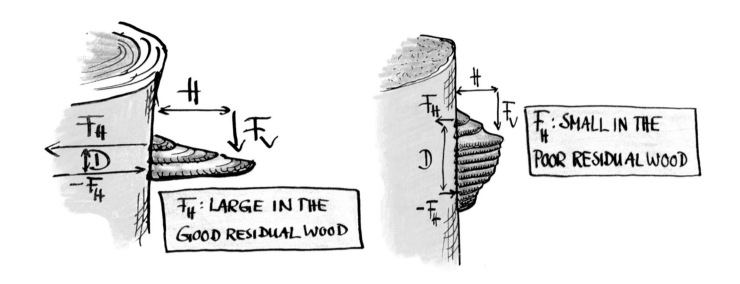

F_H: LARGE IN THE GOOD RESIDUAL WOOD

F_H: SMALL IN THE POOR RESIDUAL WOOD

$$F_V \cdot H = F_H \cdot D$$

$$F_H = F_V \cdot \frac{H}{D}$$

IF YOU DEFINE THE HEIGHT H OF THE FUNGUS FRUIT BODY AS IN THE DRAWING, AND THE VERTICAL FORCE F_v IS BENDING IT DOWNWARD, THEN SMALLER HORIZONTAL FORCES F_H WILL BE ACTING IN THE WOOD AT A SIMPLIFIED ASSUMED DISTANCE D, IF THE FRUIT BODY IS DECLINING. THAT IS THE CASE WHEN THE WOOD IS ALREADY VERY DECAYED. THE LEVER ARM H IS NO LONGER INCREASING, ONLY THE LEVER ARM D OF THE HORIZONTAL FORCES IN THE WOOD. EVEN THAT IS ACTING A LITTLE AGAINST THE TEARING OUT OF THE FRUIT BODY. IF THE LEVER ARM D IS BECOMING INCREASINGLY LARGE, THEN QUITE SMALL HORIZONTAL TEAR-OUT FORCES WILL BE PULLING ROUND ON THE WOOD. ISN'T IT AMAZING WHAT FUNGI DO?

PAULI IS SHOWING HOW THE WOOD FORCES DEVELOP. THE ROPE IS PULLING AND PAULI'S LEG IS PUSHING. THE FURTHER AWAY THE ROPE IS FROM PAULI'S LEG, THE SMALLER ARE THE HORIZONTAL FORCES IN THE WOOD.

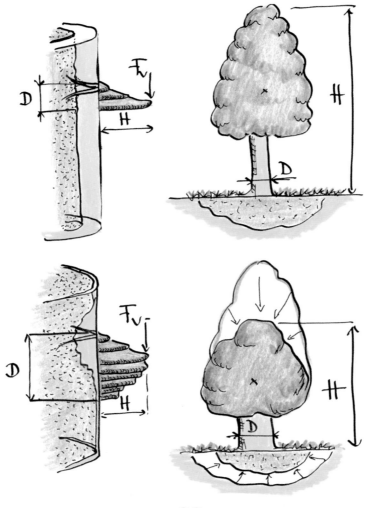

ACTUALLY, AN OLD FUNGUS FRUIT BODY DOES NOT BEHAVE VERY DIFFERENTLY FROM AN OLD TREE. IT LIMITS ITS HEIGHT H, WHICH THE TREE CAN ACTUALLY REDUCE BY DYING BACK. ALSO, LIKE THE TREE IT INCREASES ITS THICKNESS D. WITH THE FUNGUS FRUIT BODY, THE WOOD IMMEDIATELY AROUND THE ANCHORAGE POINT IS NOT DECAYED AND/OR IS REINFORCED WITH FUNGUS TISSUE. IN A TREE THAT IS DYING BACK, THE ROOT-PLATE NEAR THE STEM IS PRESERVED AS A SOIL ANCHOR. FUNGUS AND TREE HAVE A COMMON STRATEGY TO STILL BE SAFE EVEN WHEN DYING! THE H/D RATIO DECREASES!

HERE THE FUNGUS FRUIT BODY BECOMES THE WITNESS IN THE EVENT OF DAMAGE, AS IT PROVES THAT THE ACCIDENT WAS PREDICTABLE. FRUIT BODIES ALWAYS GROW WITH THE PORES DOWNWARD, I.E. GEOTROPICALLY! THE FRUIT BODY ARROWED WAS ON THE TREE BEFORE THE ACCIDENT. ITS INCREMENTS ARE DECREASING. HOWEVER, THE GEOTROPICALLY TWISTED FRUIT BODY GROWING OUT OF IT BELOW IS STILL GROWING STRONGLY. THIS IS BECAUSE COMPARTMENTALIZATION MECHANISMS COLLAPSED AFTER THE STEM BROKE, AND THE FUNGUS COULD OCCUPY NEW ZONES OF WOOD AND NOURISH ITSELF. ON THE STANDING STUMP THE WOOD IS MORE DECAYED ABOVE THAN BELOW: THE UPPER FRUIT BODY IS DECLINING GREATLY – INDEED, IF YOU UNDERSTAND ITS BODY LANGUAGE A FUNGUS FRUIT BODY IS A TALKATIVE LITTLE FELLOW.

YOU CANNOT DEFINITELY DECIDE FROM THESE FUNGUS FRUIT BODIES THAT THE ACCIDENT WAS PREDICTABLE, BECAUSE NO GEOTROPIC TWISTING OF A FRUIT BODY THAT WAS PRESENT BEFORE THE ACCIDENT IS VISIBLE ON THE FALLEN PART OF THE TREE. ALSO, THE FRUIT BODIES NOW GROWING HORIZONTALLY ON THE FALLEN STEM ARE ABOUT AS LARGE AND AT ABOUT THE SAME DISTANCE FROM THE FRACTURE AS THOSE ON THE STANDING STUMP. IT MAY VERY WELL BE THAT NO FRUIT BODY WAS VISIBLE BEFORE THE STEM BROKE. COULD SUCH FRUIT BODIES AS PAULI SEES THEM EVER ACTUALLY EXIST ON THE STANDING TREE?

103

HERE THE FUNGUS FRUIT BODIES SHOW THAT THE TREE WAS LEANING AT THE ANGLE α. BUT IT ALREADY HAD A FRUIT BODY BEFORE IT STARTED LEANING. AFTER THE LEANING, TWO NEW FRUIT BODIES FORMED BELOW THE LATER PLACES OF FRACTURE AND ONE ABOVE. THIS LATTER ONE IS NOW ON THE FALLEN PART OF THE STEM. IT PROVES THAT IT DEVELOPED BEFORE THE FRACTURE BUT AFTER THE LEANING OCCURRED, AND THAT THE ACCIDENT WAS PREDICTABLE.

AFTER AN ACCIDENT THE COURT IS OFTEN FACED WITH THE QUESTION WHETHER PIECES OF EVIDENCE HAVE BEEN MOVED. THESE FUNGUS FRUIT BODIES SHOW THAT AT LEAST ONE ROLLING MOVEMENT OF THE STEM HAS TAKEN PLACE. THE UPPER FRUIT BODY ON THE LEFT IS NO LONGER QUITE NEW BUT ITS PORES ARE NOW POINTING DOWNWARDS (GEOTROPISM!). THE STEM HAD BEEN MOVED SOME WEEKS OR MONTHS AGO, BECAUSE THE PORES OF THE LOWER FRUIT BODY IN THE LEFT-HAND PICTURE ARE POINTING UPWARDS.

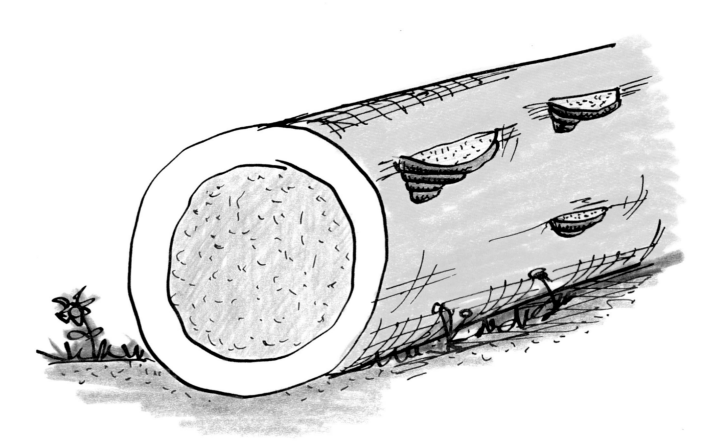

HERE THE PORES OF ALL THE FUNGUS FRUIT
BODIES ARE POINTING UPWARDS, AND
NATURALLY THIS ANNOYS THEM EXCEEDINGLY
BECAUSE THEY WANT TO LET THEIR SPORES
FALL OUT DOWNWARDS. THEREFORE THIS LOG
MUST HAVE BEEN MOVED, AND THAT MEANS
AT LEAST ROLLED, ONLY A SHORT TIME AGO.
THERE HASN'T BEEN TIME FOR EVEN A VERY
SMALL FRUIT BODY TO FORM WITH THE
CORRECT ORIENTATION, I.E. PORES DOWN.
PAULI IS PERSONALLY DEMONSTRATING THIS
EXTREMELY UNUSUAL SITUATION.

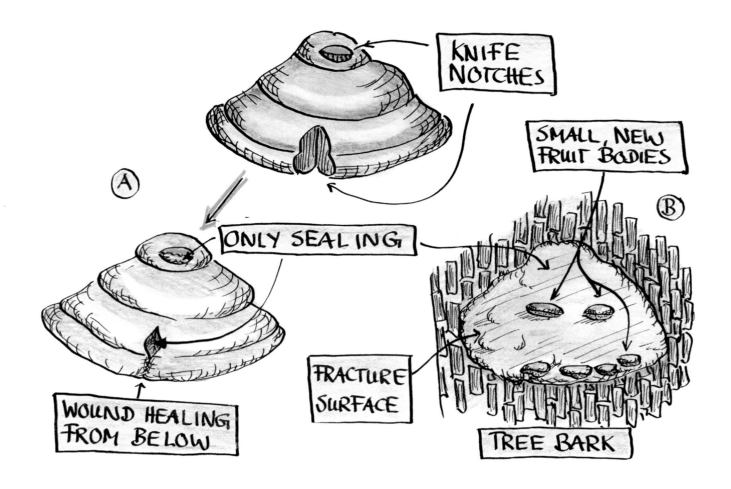

KNIFE NOTCHES

SMALL, NEW FRUIT BODIES

Ⓐ

Ⓑ

ONLY SEALING

FRACTURE SURFACE

WOUND HEALING FROM BELOW

TREE BARK

110

WE ALL KNOW THAT TREES CLOSE THEIR WOUNDS, AND THAT THEY ARE MASTERS OF SELF-REPAIR. ULTIMATELY, THEY CANNOT RUN AWAY IF THREATENED BY INJURY. BUT WHAT HAPPENS IF YOU INJURE A FUNGUS FRUIT BODY? IT WILL ALSO CLOSE THE WOUND. BUT IT LOOKS AS THOUGH IT WOULD FIRST START BY SEALING THE WOUND SURFACE, AND THEN CLOSE THE WOUND FROM BELOW LIKE A ZIP-FASTENER. FINALLY THE ACTIVE GROWTH RING WITH THE PORES IS ALSO BELOW. IF YOU TEAR A FUNGUS FRUIT BODY OFF, WHICH MAY CONSTITUTE THE REMOVAL OF EVIDENCE, THE FUNGUS TISSUE WILL FIRST SEAL THE FRACTURE SURFACE. TIGHT CLOSURE SEEMS TO BE THE SUPREME DICTATE! THEN SMALLER FRUIT BODIES MAY FORM, GROWING OUT OF THE OLD FRACTURE SURFACE OF THE LARGE FRUIT BODY. THEY ARE OFTEN FOUND BELOW, IN THE OLD GROWTH MARGIN OF THE BROKEN OFF FRUIT BODY.

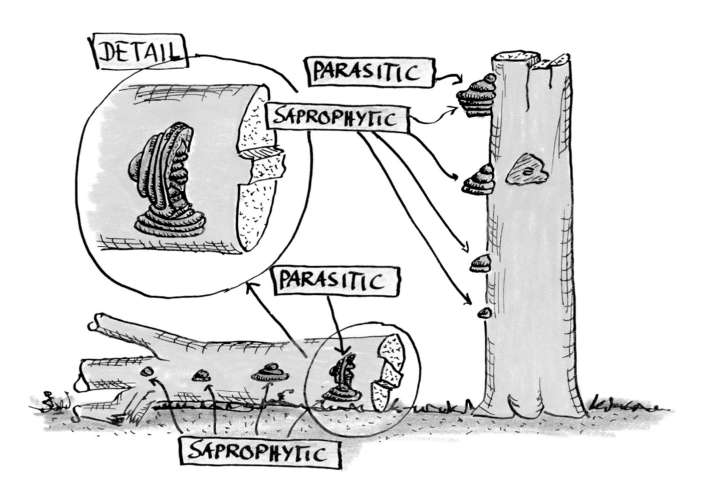

DETAIL

PARASITIC

SAPROPHYTIC

PARASITIC

SAPROPHYTIC

AFTER THIS ACCOUNT OF THE BODY LANGUAGE OF FUNGUS FRUIT BODIES, HERE ARE A FEW DETECTIVE EXERCISES ON THIS PICTURE:

1. WHERE IS THE WOOD MOST DECAYED ON THE STANDING STUMP?

2. HAVE FUNGUS FRUITING BODIES BEEN TORN OFF IT?

3. WAS THE FAILURE PREDICTABLE?

4. WHERE IS THE WOOD MOST DECAYED ON THE FALLEN PART OF THE TREE?

5. HAS THE FALLEN PART OF THE TREE BEEN MOVED AFTER THE BREAKAGE?

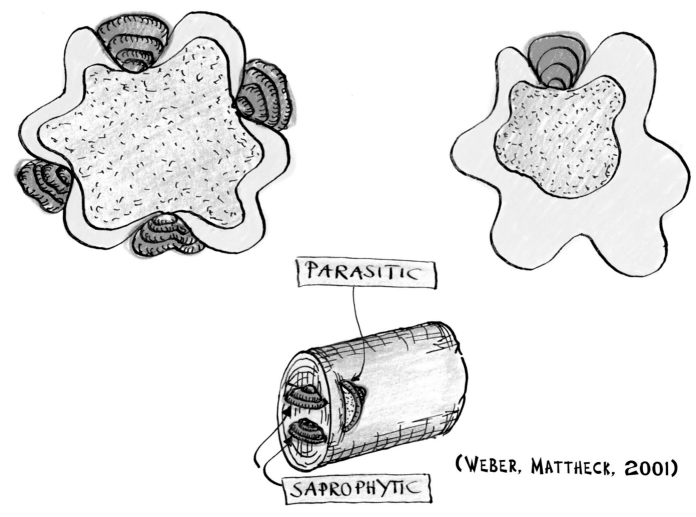

PARASITIC

SAPROPHYTIC

(WEBER, MATTHECK, 2001)

114

IF THE FUNGUS TISSUE IN THE TREE GETS IN CONTACT WITH THE OUTSIDE AIR, THIS MAY BE A STARTER SIGNAL FOR THE FORMATION OF A FUNGUS FRUIT BODY. THE RESIDUAL WALL THICKNESS IS THINNEST BETWEEN THE ROOT JUNCTIONS. THAT'S THE FIRST PLACE TO EXAMINE FOR FUNGUS FRUIT BODIES. IF THERE ARE FRUIT BODIES ALL AROUND THE BASE OF THE STEM, THE DECAY HAS SPREAD A LONG WAY. INDEED SUCH A TREE WILL OFTEN NEED TO BE FELLED. IF THE FUNGUS FRUIT BODY IS ONLY ON ONE SIDE, THE EXTENT OF THE DECAY CAN BE MEASURED BY BORING, BEFORE MAKING A PROPER JUDGEMENT ABOUT FELLING THE TREE.

NOTE: MANY ROTS WILL DECAY ONLY THE ROOTS AND DO NOT GO INTO THE STEMWOOD. THEN THE ROOTS MUST BE EXAMINED. IF A TREE IS FELLED OR ITS STEM BREAKS, FRUIT BODIES OFTEN EMERGE QUITE QUICKLY FROM THE SAWN SURFACE OR THE FRACTURE SURFACE, AND THESE THEN GROW ON THE DEAD STEM (SAPROPHYTES). FUNGI ON THE LIVING TREE ARE CALLED PARASITES. HERE TOO IT IS PROBABLY THE SUDDEN AIR CONTACT WHICH LETS THE FUNGUS FRUIT BODIES GROW.

STRONG WALL IV

MUCH RESIDUAL WOOD

LITTLE OR NO RESIDUAL WOOD

STRONG WALL IV

HOLLOW

INTERNAL FRUIT BODY

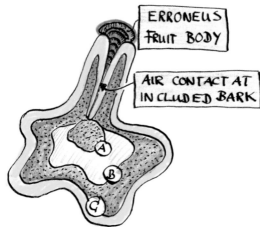

ERRONEUS FRUIT BODY

AIR CONTACT AT INCLUDED BARK

A
B
C

FUNGI OFTEN MAKE PREMATURE AIR CONTACT VIA A CRACK OR INCLUDED BARK (BOTTOM PICTURE). THEN THE FUNGUS FRUIT BODY DOES NOT INDICATE MUCH ABOUT THE EXTENT OF THE DECAY. DECAY EXTENT A, B OR C ARE EQUALLY POSSIBLE. YOU MUST BORE TO MEASURE THE EXTENT OF THE DECAY.

THE PICTURE ON THE LEFT SHOWS A TREE WITH A GOOD DECAY COMPARTMENTALIZATION. THE SO-CALLED WALL IV, PRODUCED BY THE TREE, OFTEN SEPARATES THE SOUND WOOD SAFELY FROM THE DECAYED WOOD FOR A LONG TIME (SHIGO, MARX 1977). THE FUNGUS CAN'T GET AT THIS COMPARTMENTALIZED WOOD, IT LEAVES THE HOST AND MAKES A FRUIT BODY IN THE WOUND OPENING: THE OLD ENTRANCE IS NOW THE EXIT AND ESCAPE PATH TO THE NEW HOST. IF THE OLD WOUND IS CLOSED, AS IN THE PICTURE ON THE RIGHT, AND THE FUNGUS TISSUE IS LOCKED IN BY THE WALL IV, THERE IS ONLY ONE SOLUTION LEFT: TO FORM A FRUIT BODY INWARDS WITH ONLY THE SMALLEST PROSPECT OF REACHING NEW HOSTS.

EXPERIMENTAL APPENDIX:
THE PERFORATED PLATE AS INSTRUCTOR

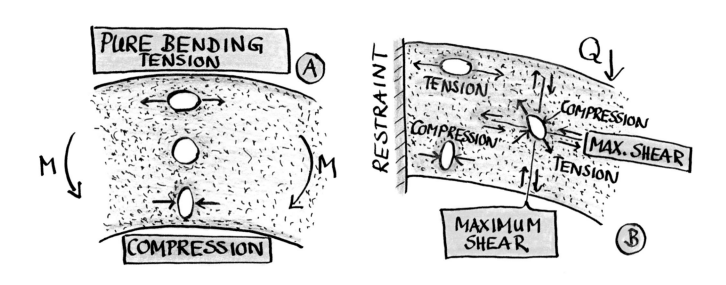

PAULI HAS GREAT EXPERIMENTS WITH PERFORATED PLATES OF VERY ELASTIC MATERIAL, BECAUSE TENSION, COMPRESSION AND SHEAR CAN BE DEMONSTRATED WITHOUT LABORIOUS CALCULATIONS. THE HOLES IN THE PLATES ARE DEFORMED LONGITUDINALLY IN THE TENSION DIRECTION, TRANSVERSELY WITH COMPRESSION LOADING (JUST LIKE PAULI'S MOUTH!), AND UNDER SHEAR THE CIRCULAR HOLES BECOME OBLIQUELY ALIGNED LONG HOLES. FIG. A SHOWS PURE BENDING, AND THERE ARE NO SHEAR STRESSES BY A TRANSVERSE FORCE. THEREFORE IN FIG. A THE MIDDLE HOLE REMAINS CIRCULAR, FOR THE BENDING STRESSES ON THE NEUTRAL FIBRES OF THE BENDING ARE ZERO. IN CONTRAST, IN FIG. B THE TRANSVERSE FORCE PRODUCES BENDING AND SHEAR STRESSES. THE LATTER ARE GREATEST LONGITUDINALLY AND TRANSVERSELY TO THE BEAM AXIS AT THE MIDDLE HOLE. INCLINED AT 45° TO THESE PLANES OF MAXIMUM SHEAR THERE IS COMPRESSION AND TENSION, WHICH NEATLY EXPLAINS THE OBLIQUE LONG HOLE.

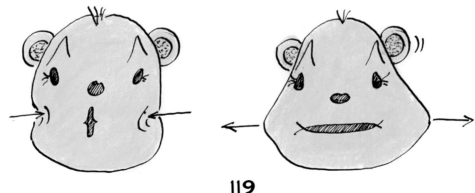

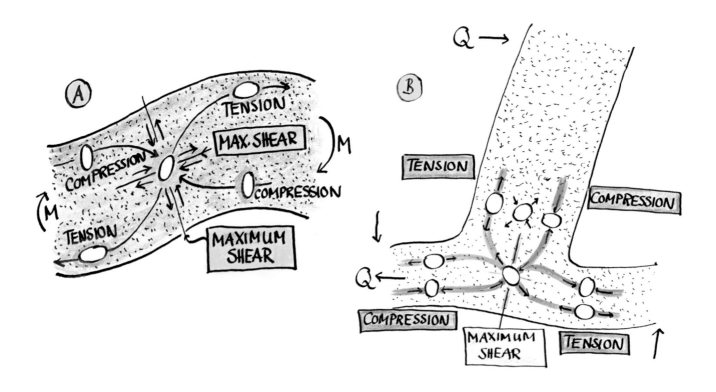

HIGH SHEAR STRESSES ALSO OCCUR IN THE TURNING POINT OF A BENDING LINE, WHERE THE BENDING MOMENT REVERSES ITS DIRECTION. THERE TENSION AND COMPRESSION CHANGE SIDES OF THE BEAM, AND THE LINE OF TENSION CROSSES THE LINE OF COMPRESSION AT THE TURNING POINT (FIG. A). HIGH SHEAR STRESSES OCCUR BETWEEN THEM. YOU CAN SEE CLEARLY HOW THE LONG HOLE IS OBLIQUE AT THE CROSSING POINT. THE SHEAR STRESSES RIGHT DOWN AT THE BASE OF THE STEM IN FIG. B CAN ALSO BE EXPLAINED SIMILARLY. THE ROOT ON THE WINDWARD (LEFT) SIDE IS BENT DOWN, AND THE ROOT ON THE LEE-SIDE (RIGHT) IS BENT UP. THE TURNING POINT OF THE BENDING LINE WITH THE HIGH SHEAR STRESSES IS EXACTLY IN THE BASE OF THE STEM. THIS DANGEROUS LOCALIZED SHEAR MAXIMUM IS ONE OF THE WEAKEST SPOTS INSIDE A TREE. ACCORDINGLY, SHEAR CRACKS USUALLY DEVELOP DOWN IN THE STEM BASE AND THEN RUN UPWARDS. IF YOU MAKE A LARGE NUMBER OF HOLES IN THE PLATE, YOU WILL EVEN SEE THAT FORCE-FLOW DISTRIBUTIONS CAN BE RECOGNIZED.

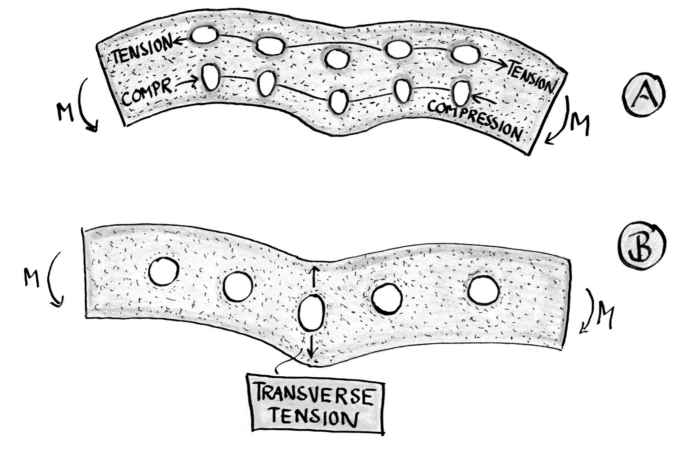

122

IF YOU BEND A CURVED COMPONENT STRAIGHT, IT CAN SPLIT LONGITUDINALLY (HAZARD BEAM). THE DISTRIBUTION OF THE LONGITUDINAL TENSILE AND COMPRESSIVE STRESSES CAN BE CLEARLY SEEN IN FIG. A. IF YOU WISH TO INVESTIGATE THE TRANSVERSE STRESSES WHICH CAUSE SPLITTING, THEN THE HOLES MUST BE POSITIONED IN THE MIDDLE OF THE BEAM WHERE THE BENDING STRESSES ARE SMALL. THERE YOU CAN SEE HOW THE MIDDLE HOLE IS PULLED TRANSVERSELY TO THE BEAM AXIS IN THE REGION OF THE CURVATURE, WHICH CAN SPLIT THE WOOD (FIG. B). BELOW, A WOODEN MODEL OF A HAZARD BEAM SHOWS WHAT THE SPLIT BEAM LOOKS LIKE.

THIS RING (HOLLOW TREE) DEFORMED BY CROSS-SECTIONAL FLATTENING HAS FOUR TURNING POINTS IN ITS BENDING LINE. THE PLACES OF HIGHEST SHEAR STRESS CAN BE CLEARLY SEEN (BLUE HOLES), WHERE TENSION AND COMPRESSION CROSS. THEY LIE PRECISELY BETWEEN THE PLACES OF HIGHEST BENDING STRESSES, WHERE THE HOLES ARE MAXIMALLY WIDENED BY TENSION AND MAXIMALLY SQUEEZED BY COMPRESSION. ON THE RIGHT IS A WOOD MODEL WHICH HAS RUPTURED AT THE PLACES OF HIGHEST TANGENTIAL TENSILE STRESS.

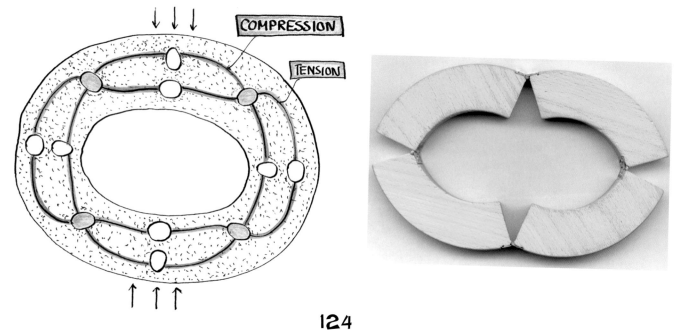

SO, DEAR FRIENDS, THERE YOU ARE. YOU HAVE NOW FOLLOWED ME THROUGH A DOORWAY INTO THE STUDY OF MECHANICS. THANK YOU FOR YOUR COURAGE AND YOUR PATIENCE! THE BOOK IS NOW AT AN END – BUT WE ARE NOT GOING TO PART, FOR NOW WE HAVE A FIELD OF WORK IN COMMON:

MECHANICS!

WE'LL SEE EACH OTHER AGAIN – FOR CERTAIN!

PAULI

LITERATURE CITED:

J. D. CURREY: THE MECHANICAL ADAPTATIONS OF BONE, PRINCETON UNIVERSITY PRESS, GUILDFORT, 1984

J. D. CURREY, R. MC N. ALEXANDER: THE THICKNESS OF THE WALLS OF TUBULAR BONES, J. ZOOL. LOND. (A) (1985) 206, P. 453-468

K. GÖTZ: THE INTERNAL OPTIMISATION OF TREES AS A PATTERN FOR TECHNICAL FIBRE COMPOSITES - A LOCAL APPROXIMATION, SCIENTIFIC REPORT, FZKA 6552, 2000 (DOCTORAL THESIS), IN GERMAN

M. R. JACOBS: A STUDY OF THE EFFECT OF SWAY ON TREES, COMMONWEALTH FORESTRY BUREAU, BULLETIN NO. 26, P. 7-18, 1939

G.W. LAVERS: THE STRENGTH PROPERTIES OF TIMBER, HMSO, LONDON, 3RD EDITION 1983

M. LEDERMANN: CONTRIBUTIONS TO THE OPTIMISATION OF FIBRE COMPOSITES FOLLOWING NATURE'S PATTERN, DOCTORAL THESIS AT THE MECHANICAL ENGINEERING FACULTY, KARLSRUHE UNIVERSITY, 2002, IN GERMAN

C. MATTHECK, K. BETHGE, I. TESARI, R. KAPPEL: A NEW FAILURE CRITERION FOR NON-DECAYED SOLITARY TREES UNDAMAGED BY DECAY, SCIENTIFIC REPORT, FZKA 6666, 2001, IN GERMAN

K.H. WEBER, C. MATTHECK: POCKET BOOK FOR WOOD DECAY IN TREES, PUBL. FORSCHUNGSZENTRUM KARLSRUHE GMBH, 2001, IN GERMAN

A. Shigo, H. Marx: Compartmentalization of decay in trees, Agriculture information Bull, no. 405, 1977, Forest Service, U.S.Department of Agriculture

FURTHER READING:

C. Mattheck: Design in nature: Learning from trees, Publ. Springer, Heidelberg 1998

C. Mattheck: Stupsi explains the tree: A hedgehog teaches the body language of trees, Publ. Forschungszentrum Karlsruhe GmbH, 3rd enlarged edition 1999

C. Mattheck, H. Kubler: Wood – the internal optimization of trees, Publ. Springer, Heidelberg, 2nd edition 1997

A. Shigo, A new tree biology, Durham, 2nd edition 1989

R. Harris, J. Clark, N. Matheny: Arboriculture, Prentice Hall, New Jersey, 3rd edition 1999

W. Young, R. Budynas: Roark´s formulas for stress and strain, Mc Graw Hill, New York, 7th edition 2002

symbol	meaning	unit	abbreviation
Q	force	newton	N
F_V	vertical force	newton	N
F_H	horizontal force	newton	N
M, M_B	bending moment	newton·metre	Nm
M_T	torsional moment	newton·metre	Nm
M	mass	kilogram	kg
σ (SIGMA)	normal stress	megapascal	MPa=N/mm^2
τ (TAU)	shear stress	megapascal	MPa=N/mm^2
ℓ	lever-arm-length	metre	m
H	height	metre	m
D	diameter	metre	m
R	radius	metre	m
A	area	square metre	m^2
T	oscillation period	second	s
f	frequency	1/second or hertz	1/s=Hz
c	stiffness	newton/metre	N/m

for conversions

centi=1/100
milli=1/1000
kilo =1000
mega=10^6

PAULI THE BEAR IS A LOVABLE SEDUCER. SO CLEVERLY, SO CLEARLY DOES HE INTRODUCE THE MECHANICS OF TREES THAT THE READER DOES NOT REALIZE THAT THIS IS A DIFFICULT FIELD. ON THE CONTRARY, IT SUDDENLY BECOMES OBVIOUS WHY TREES BEHAVE IN CERTAIN WAYS AND NOT OTHERS, AND THAT THEY CAN BE CALCULATED.
ONE THING IS CLEAR: PAULI LOVES TREES AND - RATHER SECRETLY - MECHANICS TOO.

PROF. DR. DIETMAR GROSS
INSTITUTE FOR MECHANICS, TECHNICAL UNIVERSITY, DARMSTADT, GERMANY

WITH SPIRIT, HEART AND SOME CUNNING, THE BOOK ENTICES THE READER INTO MECHANICS ON THE TRAIL OF PAULI THE BEAR. BIOLOGISTS, ARBORICULTURISTS OR FORESTERS WHO OPEN A 'HARD' BOOK ON MECHANICS WILL USUALLY PUT IT AWAY AGAIN WITH A SHUDDER AFTER THE FIRST GLANCE AT THE ARID WORLD OF FORMULAE.
I AM CONVINCED THAT PAULI THE BEAR SUCCEEDS IN TAKING THE READER BY THE HAND AND INTRODUCING HIM GENTLY INTO A MORE QUANTITATIVE UNDERSTANDING OF LIVING STRUCTURES WHICH - LIKE TREES - CAN ALSO BE OUR FRIENDS.

PROF. DR. DIETRICH MUNZ
INSTITUTE FOR RELIABILITY AND FAILURE ANALYSIS IN MECHANICAL ENGINEERING, KARLSRUHE UNIVERSITY, GERMANY

FOR INFORMATION ON SEMINARS ON

- BIOMECHANICS OF TREES
- TREE DIAGNOSIS
- WOOD DECAYS AND TREE FUNGI

ERIKA KOCH

TEL.: ++49-711-715 7564
FAX.: ++49-711-715 6410

WE'LL BE GLAD TO HELP!